The ABC
of European Union law

by Professor Klaus-Dieter Borchardt

The content of this publication does not necessarily reflect the official position of the European Union. The information and opinions contained herein are the sole responsibility of the author.

Photo credits

Listed below are the storage locations of the illustrations reproduced and/or the source used, together with the copyright holders.

Every effort has been made to locate the holders of the rights of the various illustrations and photographs reproduced. If you have any questions, please contact the publisher:

Publications Office of the European Union
2, rue Mercier
2985 Luxembourg
LUXEMBOURG

Pages 8, 23, 35, 56, 67, 84, 94, 116 and 124: European Commission Media Library, Brussels
© European Union, 2010

Europe Direct is a service to help you find answers to your questions about the European Union.

Freephone number (*):

00 800 6 7 8 9 10 11

(*) Certain mobile telephone operators do not allow access to 00 800 numbers, or these calls may be billed.

More information on the European Union is available on the Internet (http://europa.eu).

Cataloguing data can be found at the end of this publication.

Luxembourg: Publications Office of the European Union, 2010

ISBN 978-92-78-40525-0
doi:10.2830/13717

Printed in Germany

PRINTED ON ELEMENTAL CHLORINE-FREE BLEACHED PAPER

NOTE TO THE READER

The ABC of European Union law takes account of the modifications made to the European Treaties by the Treaty of Lisbon. Unless there is a direct citation, or the historical context demands, the articles cited refer exclusively to the consolidated versions of the European Treaties (*Official Journal of the European Union* C 83 of 30 March 2010). The information given in this edition is correct as at March 2010.

Contents

Foreword

The legal order created by the European Union (EU) has already become an established component of our political life and society. Each year, on the basis of the Union Treaties, thousands of decisions are taken that crucially affect the EU Member States and the lives of their citizens. Individuals have long since ceased to be merely citizens of their country, town or district; they are also Union citizens. For this reason alone, it is of crucial importance that they should be informed about the legal order that affects their daily lives. Yet the complexities of the Union's structure and its legal order are not easy to grasp. This is partly due to the wording of the Treaties themselves, which is often somewhat obscure, with implications which are not easy to appreciate. An additional factor is the unfamiliarity of many concepts with which the Treaties seek to master the situation. The following pages are an attempt to clarify the structure of the Union and the supporting pillars of the European legal order, and thus help to lessen any lack of understanding among the citizens of the EU.

7 May 1948, The Hague.
Winston Churchill is warmly welcomed at the
Congress of Europe. The former British Prime
Minister, and leader of the opposition at the time,
chaired the inaugural session of the Congress. On
19 September 1946, he had called for European
unity in his Zurich address.

From Paris to Lisbon, via Rome, Maastricht, Amsterdam and Nice

Until shortly after the end of the Second World War our concept of the state and our political life had developed almost entirely on the basis of national constitutions and laws. It was on this basis that the rules of conduct binding not only on citizens and parties in our democratic states but also on the state and its organs were created. It took the complete collapse of Europe and its political and economic decline to create the conditions for a new beginning and give a fresh impetus to the idea of a new European order.

In overall terms, moves towards unification in Europe since the Second World War have created a confusing mixture of numerous and complex organisations that are difficult to keep track of. For example, the OECD (Organisation for Economic Cooperation and Development), WEU (Western European Union), NATO (North Atlantic Treaty Organisation), the Council of Europe and the European Union coexist without any real links between them. The number of member countries in these various organisations ranges from 10 (WEU) to 47 (Council of Europe).

This variety of organisations only acquires a logical structure if we look at their specific aims. They can be divided into three main groups.

First group: the Euro-Atlantic organisations

The Euro-Atlantic organisations came into being as a result of the alliance between the United States of America and Europe after the Second World War. It was no coincidence that the first European organisation of the post-war period, the OEEC (Organisation for European Economic Cooperation), founded in 1948, was created at the initiative of the United States. The US Secretary of State at the time, George Marshall, called on the countries of Europe in 1947 to join forces in rebuilding their economies and promised

American help. This came in the form of the Marshall Plan, which provided the foundation for the rapid reconstruction of western Europe. At first, the main aim of the OEEC was to liberalise trade between countries. In 1960, when the USA and Canada became members, a further objective was added, namely to promote economic progress in the Third World through development aid. The OEEC then became the OECD.

In 1949, NATO was founded as a military alliance with the United States and Canada. In 1954, the Western European Union (WEU) was created to strengthen security policy cooperation between the countries of Europe. It brought together the countries that had concluded the Brussels Treaty (Belgium, France, Luxembourg, the Netherlands and the United Kingdom) with the addition of the Federal Republic of Germany and Italy. Greece, Spain and Portugal have also become members. The WEU marked the beginnings of a security and defence policy in Europe in 1954. However, its role has not developed further, since the majority of its powers have been transferred to other international institutions, notably NATO, the Council of Europe and the EU. The WEU has retained the responsibility for collective defence, a role which has yet to be transferred to the EU.

SECOND GROUP: COUNCIL OF EUROPE AND OSCE

The feature common to the second group of European organisations is that they are structured to enable as many countries as possible to participate. At the same time, there was an awareness that these organisations would not go beyond customary international cooperation.

These organisations include the Council of Europe, which was founded as a political institution on 5 May 1949. Its statute does not make any reference to moves towards a federation or union, nor does it provide for the transfer or merging of sovereign rights. Decisions on all important questions require unanimity, which means that every country has a power of veto; the same set-up is to be found in the United Nations (UN) Security Council. The Council of Europe is therefore designed only with international cooperation in mind. Numerous conventions have been concluded by the Council in the fields of economics, culture, social policy and law. The most important — and best-known — of these is the European Convention for the Protection of Human Rights and Fundamental Freedoms (European Convention on Human Rights or ECHR) of 4 November 1950. The convention not only enabled a minimum standard for the safeguarding of human rights to be laid down for the member countries; it also established a system of legal protection which enables the bodies established in Strasbourg under it (the European Commission on Human Rights and the European Court of Human Rights) to condemn violations of human rights in the member countries.

This group of organisations also includes the Organisation for Security and Cooperation in Europe (OSCE), founded in 1994 as the successor to the Conference on Security and Cooperation in Europe. The OSCE is bound by the principles and aims set out in the 1975 Helsinki Final Act and the 1990 Charter of Paris. Alongside measures to build up trust between the countries of Europe, these aims also include the creation of a 'safety net' to enable conflicts to be settled by peaceful means. As events of the recent past have shown, Europe still has a long way to go in this respect.

THIRD GROUP: EUROPEAN UNION

The third group of European organisations comprises the European Union. The feature that is completely new in the EU and distinguishes it from the usual type of international association of states is that the Member States have ceded some of their sovereign rights to the EU and have conferred on the Union powers to act independently. In exercising these powers, the EU is able to issue sovereign acts which have the same force as laws in individual states.

The foundation stone of the European Union was laid by the then French Foreign Minister Robert Schuman in his declaration of 9 May 1950, in which he put forward the plan he had worked out with Jean Monnet to bring Europe's coal and steel industries together to form a European Coal and Steel Community. This would, he declared, constitute a historic initiative for an 'organised and vital Europe', which was 'indispensable for civilisation' and without which the 'peace of the world could not be maintained'. The 'Schuman Plan' finally became a reality with the conclusion of the founding Treaty of the European Coal and Steel Community (ECSC) by the six founding States (Belgium, Germany, France, Italy, Luxembourg and the Netherlands) on 18 April 1951 in Paris (Treaty of Paris) and its entry into force on 23 July 1952. This Community was established for a period of 50 years, and was 'integrated' into the European Community when its founding Treaty expired on 23 July 2002. A further development came some years later with the Treaties of Rome of 25 March 1957, which created the European Economic Community (EEC) and the European Atomic Energy Community (Euratom); these began their work when the Treaties entered into force on 1 January 1958.

The creation of the European Union by means of the Treaty of Maastricht marked a further step along the path to the political unification of Europe. Although the Treaty was signed in Maastricht on 7 February 1992, a number of obstacles in the ratification process (approval by the people of Denmark only after a second referendum; legal action in Germany to have Parliament's approval of the Treaty declared unconstitutional) meant that it did not enter into force until 1 November 1993. The Treaty referred to itself as 'a new stage in the process of creating an ever closer union among the peoples of Europe'. It contained the instrument establishing the European Union, although it did not bring this process to completion. It was a first step on the path leading ultimately to a European constitutional system.

Further development came in the form of the Treaties of Amsterdam and Nice, which entered into force on 1 May 1999 and 1 February 2003. The aim of these reforms was to preserve the EU's capacity for effective action in a Union enlarged from 15 to 27 or more members. The two Treaties therefore focused on institutional reforms and, compared with previous reforms, the political will to deepen European integration in Nice was relatively weak.

The subsequent criticism from several quarters resulted in the start of a debate on the future of the EU and its institutional set-up. As a result, on 5 December 2001 in Laeken (Belgium), the Heads of State or Government adopted a Declaration on the Future of the European Union, in which the EU undertook to become more democratic, transparent and effective and to open the road to a constitution. The first step to achieving this goal was taken by setting up a European convention, chaired by the former President of France, Valéry Giscard d'Estaing, with the remit of drafting a European constitution. On 18 July 2003 the Chairman, on behalf of the convention, officially submitted the draft of the Treaty drawn up by the convention to the President of the European Council. This draft was adopted, with certain amendments, by the Heads of State or Government on 17 and 18 July in

Brussels after the accession of the 10 new Member States on 1 May 2004 and the European Parliament elections in mid-June 2004.

The constitution was intended to turn the European Union and the European Community as we knew them into a new, single European Union based on a single Constitutional Treaty. Only the European Atomic Energy Community would continue to exist as a separate Community — although it would continue to be closely associated with the European Union.

However, this attempt at a constitution failed in the ratification process. After the initial votes were positive in 13 of the 25 Member States, the Treaty was rejected in referendums in France (54.68 % against, from a turnout of 69.34 %) and the Netherlands (61.7 % against, from a turnout of 63 %).

Following a period of reflection of almost two years, a new package of reforms was launched in the first half of 2007. This reform package represented a move away from the idea of a European constitution under which all existing Treaties would be revoked and replaced by a single text called the 'Treaty establishing a Constitution for Europe'. Instead, a Reform Treaty was drawn up, which, like the Treaties of Maastricht, Amsterdam and Nice before it, made fundamental changes to the existing EU Treaties in order to strengthen the EU's capacity to act within and outside the Union, increase its democratic legitimacy and enhance the efficiency of EU action overall. In line with tradition, this Reform Treaty was called the Treaty of Lisbon.

The Treaty was drafted unusually quickly, chiefly due to the fact that the Heads of State or Government themselves set out in detail in the conclusions of the meeting of the European Council of 21 and 22 June 2007 in Brussels how and to what extent the changes negotiated at the Intergovernmental Conference of 2004 were to be incorporated into the existing Treaties. Their approach was unusual in that they did not limit themselves to general directions to be implemented by an Intergovernmental Conference, but themselves drew up the structure and content of the changes to be made, and indeed often set out the exact wording of a provision. The main points of contention were the delimitation of competences between the Union and the Member States, the future of the common foreign and security policy, the new role of the national parliaments in the integration process, the incorporation of the Charter of Fundamental Rights into Union law and possible progress in the area of police and judicial cooperation in criminal matters.

As a result, the Intergovernmental Conference convened in 2007 had little room for manoeuvre and was only empowered to implement the required changes technically. The work of the Intergovernmental Conference was completed by the 18 and 19 October 2007, and obtained the political approval of the European Council, which was meeting informally in Lisbon at the same time. Finally, the Treaty was formally signed by the Heads of State or Government of the 27 Member States of the EU on 13 December 2007 in Lisbon.

However, the ratification process for this Treaty proved extremely difficult. Although the Lisbon Treaty, unlike the Treaty establishing a Constitution for Europe, was successfully ratified in France and the Netherlands, it initially fell at the hurdle of a first referendum in Ireland on 12 June 2008 (53.4 % against, in a turnout of 53.1 %). Only after a number of legal assurances on the (limited) scope of the new Treaty were Irish citizens called to vote in a second referendum on the Lisbon Treaty in October 2009. This time the Treaty received the broad support of the Irish population (67.1 % for, in a turnout of 59 %). The success of the referendum in Ireland also opened the way for ratification of the Lisbon Treaty in Poland and the Czech Republic. In Poland, President Kaczyński had made signature of the instrument of ratification dependent on a favourable outcome in the Irish referendum. The Czech President, Václav Klaus, also initially wanted to wait for the Irish referendum, but then made his signature of the instrument of ratification dependent on a guarantee that the 'Beneš decrees' of 1945, which disallowed claims to land in areas of the Czech Republic that were formerly German, would remain unaffected by the Lisbon Treaty, and in particular the Charter of Fundamental Rights incorporated into the EU Treaty. Once a solution had been found to this demand, the Czech President signed the instrument of ratification on 3 November 2009. Thus, the ratification process was completed in the last of the 27 Member States, and the Treaty of Lisbon could enter into force on 1 December 2009.

The Treaty of Lisbon merges the European Union and the European Community into a single European Union. The word 'Community' is replaced throughout by the word 'Union'. The Union replaces and succeeds the European Community. However, Union law is still shaped by the following three Treaties.

Treaty on European Union

The Treaty on European Union (EU Treaty — 'TEU') has been completely restructured into the following six titles: Common provisions (I), Provisions on democratic principles (II), Provisions on institutions (III), Provisions on enhanced cooperation (IV), General provisions on the Union's external action and specific provisions on the common foreign and security policy (V) and Final provisions (VI).

Treaty on the Functioning of the European Union

The Treaty on the Functioning of the European Union ('TFEU') has been developed from the Treaty establishing the European Community. It has more or less the same structure as the EC Treaty. The main changes concern the external action of the EU and the introduction of new chapters, in particular on energy policy, police and judicial cooperation in criminal matters, space, sport and tourism.

Treaty establishing the European Atomic Energy Community

The Treaty establishing the European Atomic Energy Community (EAEC Treaty — 'Euratom Treaty') has been amended at different stages. In each case, the specific amendments have been made in protocols annexed to the Treaty of Lisbon.

The TEU and the TFEU have the same legal standing. This explicit legal clarification is necessary, since the new title of the former EC Treaty ('Treaty on the Functioning of the EU') and the levels of regulation in both Treaties give the impression that the TEU is a sort of constitution or basic treaty, whilst the TFEU is intended as an implementing treaty. However, the TEU and the TFEU are not constitutional in nature. The terms used in the Treaties overall reflect this change of approach from the former draft constitution. The expression 'constitution' is no longer used; the 'EU foreign minister' is referred to as the 'High Representative of the Union for Foreign Affairs and Security Policy'; and the definitions of 'law' and 'framework law' have been abandoned. The amended Treaties also contain no articles referring to the symbols of the EU, such as the flag, anthem or motto. The primacy of EU law is not explicitly laid down in a treaty, but is derived, as before, from the case-law of the Court of Justice of the European Union, and this case-law is referred to in an explanatory declaration.

The Treaty of Lisbon also abandons the EU's 'three pillars'. The first pillar, consisting essentially of the single market and the EC policies, is merged with the second pillar, consisting of the common foreign and security policy, and the third pillar, covering police and judicial cooperation in criminal matters. However, the special procedures relating to the common foreign and security policy, including European defence, remain in force; the Intergovernmental Conference declarations attached to the Treaty underline the special nature of this policy area and the particular responsibilities of the Member States in this respect.

The EU currently has 27 Member States. These comprise first of all the six founder members of the EEC, namely Belgium, Germany (including the territory of the former GDR following the unification of the two Germanies on 3 October 1990), France, Italy, Luxembourg and the Netherlands. On 1 January 1973, Denmark (now excluding Greenland, which in a referendum in February 1982 voted by a narrow majority not to remain in the EC), Ireland and the United Kingdom joined the Community; Norway's planned accession was rejected in a referendum in October 1972 (with 53.5 % against EC membership). The 'enlargement to the south' was begun with the accession of Greece on 1 January 1981 and completed on 1 January 1986 with the accession of Spain and Portugal. The next enlargement took place on 1 January 1995 when Austria, Finland and Sweden joined the EU. In Norway, a referendum led to a repeat of the outcome 22 years before, with a small majority (52.4 %) against Norwegian membership of the EU. On 1 May 2004 the Baltic States of Estonia, Latvia and Lithuania, the east and central European States of the Czech Republic, Hungary, Poland, Slovenia and Slovakia and the two Mediterranean islands of Cyprus and Malta joined the EU. Only a little over two years later, the enlargement to the east was completed for the time being with the accession of Bulgaria and Romania on 1 January 2007. This extended the number of Member States from 15 to 27 and increased the EU population by around 90 million, bringing it to 474 million. This historic enlargement of the EU is the centrepiece of a long process leading to the reunification of a Europe that had been divided for over half a century by the Iron Curtain and the cold war. Above all, it reflects the desire to bring peace, stability and economic prosperity to a unified European continent.

Further accession negotiations are under way, notably with Turkey, which submitted its application for membership on 14 April 1987. However, relations between the EU and Turkey go back further than this. As long ago as 1963, Turkey and the EEC entered into an association agreement which referred to the prospect of membership. In 1995, a customs union was formed and, in Helsinki in December 1999, the European Council decided to grant Turkey officially the status of an accession candidate. This was a reflection of the belief that the country had the basic features of a democratic system, although it still displayed serious shortcomings in terms of human rights and the protection of minorities. In December 2004, on the basis of the Commission's recommendation, the European Council finally gave the go-ahead for the opening of accession negotiations with Turkey; these negotiations have been ongoing since October 2005. The ultimate aim of these negotiations is accession, but there is no guarantee that this aim will be achieved. There is also agreement within the EU that accession is not possible before 2014. Any such accession must be thoroughly prepared to allow for smooth integration and to avoid endangering the achievements of over 50 years of European integration. Other candidates for accession are Croatia, where the path to the start of accession negotiations was cleared in October 2005, and the former Yugoslav Republic of Macedonia, which was given official candidate country status in December 2005 without an actual date for the start of negotiations being set. Iceland submitted an application for membership on 17 July 2009. On 24 February 2010 the European Commission recommended that the Council open accession negotiations with Iceland.

The EU is now also working resolutely for new enlargements in the western Balkan region. It has decided to apply the same methodology to the western Balkan countries as it used previously for the new Member States. An extended stabilisation and association process therefore remains the overall framework for the progression of the countries of the western Balkans, all the way to their accession. A first important step in this direction is the 'European partnerships' established with Albania, Bosnia and Herzegovina and Serbia and Montenegro, including Kosovo (¹). The role of the European

---

(¹) *Pursuant to UN Security Council Resolution 1244 of 10 June 1999.*

partnerships, updated as necessary, is to assist the western Balkan countries in preparing for membership within a coherent framework and in developing action plans with timetables of reforms and details in terms of the means by which they intend to address the requirements for further integration into the EU.

Provision has also been made for withdrawal from the EU. A withdrawal clause has been incorporated into the EU Treaty, allowing a Member State to leave. There are no conditions for such a withdrawal from the Union; all that is required is an agreement between the EU and the Member State concerned on the arrangements for its withdrawal. If such agreement cannot be reached, the withdrawal becomes effective without any agreement two years after the notification of the intention to withdraw. However, there is no provision for expulsion of a Member State from the EU for serious and persistent breaches of the Treaties.

Fundamental values of the European Union

Article 2 of the TEU (values of the Union)

The Union is founded on the values of respect for human dignity, freedom, democracy, equality, the rule of law and respect for human rights, including the rights of persons belonging to minorities. These values are common to the Member States in a society in which pluralism, non-discrimination, tolerance, justice, solidarity and equality between women and men prevail.

Article 3 of the TEU (aims of the Union)

1. The Union's aim is to promote peace, its values and the well-being of its peoples.

2. The Union shall offer its citizens an area of freedom, security and justice without internal frontiers, in which the free movement of persons is ensured in conjunction with appropriate measures with respect to external border controls, asylum, immigration and the prevention and combating of crime.

3. The Union shall establish an internal market. It shall work for the sustainable development of Europe based on balanced economic growth and price stability, a highly competitive social market economy, aiming at full employment and social progress, and a high level of protection and improvement of the quality of the environment. It shall promote scientific and technological advance.

It shall combat social exclusion and discrimination, and shall promote social justice and protection, equality between women and men, solidarity between generations and protection of the rights of the child.

It shall promote economic, social and territorial cohesion, and solidarity among Member States.

It shall respect its rich cultural and linguistic diversity, and shall ensure that Europe's cultural heritage is safeguarded and enhanced.

4. The Union shall establish an economic and monetary union whose currency is the euro.

5. In its relations with the wider world, the Union shall uphold and promote its values and interests and contribute to the protection of its citizens. It shall contribute to peace, security, the sustainable development of the Earth, solidarity and mutual respect among peoples, free and fair trade, eradication of poverty and the protection of human rights, in particular the rights of the child, as well as to the strict observance and the development of international law, including respect for the principles of the United Nations Charter.

[…]

The foundations of a united Europe were laid on fundamental ideas and values to which the Member States also subscribe and which are translated into practical reality by the Community's operational institutions. These are lasting peace, unity, equality, freedom, solidarity and security. The EU's avowed aims are to safeguard the principles of liberty, democracy and the rule of law which are shared by all the Member States, and to protect fundamental and human rights. These values are also those to be aimed for by states wishing to join the EU in the future. In addition, penalties can be applied to any Member State which seriously and persistently breaches these values and principles. If the Heads of State or Government, acting on a proposal by one third of the Member States or by the Commission, and after obtaining the assent of the European Parliament, declare that a serious and persistent breach of the EU's underlying values and principles has occurred, the Council may, acting by a qualified majority, suspend certain of the rights deriving from the application of the EU Treaty and the Treaty on the Functioning of the European Union to the Member State in question, including voting rights in the Council. On the other hand, the obligations on the Member State in question under the Treaties continue to be binding. Particular account is taken of the effects on the rights and obligations of citizens and enterprises.

THE **EU** AS GUARANTOR OF PEACE

There is no greater motivation for European unification than the desire for peace. In the last century, two world wars were waged in Europe between countries that are now Member States of the European Union. Thus, a policy for Europe means at the same time a policy for peace, and the establishment of the EU simultaneously created the centrepiece of a framework for peace in Europe that renders a war between the Member States impossible. Fifty years of peace in Europe are proof of this. The more European States that join the EU, the stronger this framework of peace will become. The last two enlargements of the EU, including 12 predominantly east and central European States, have made a major contribution in this respect.

UNITY AND EQUALITY AS THE RECURRING THEME

Unity is the recurring theme. The present-day problems can be mastered only if European countries move forward along the path that leads them to unity. Many people take the view that without European integration, without the European Union, it would not be possible to secure peace (both in Europe and worldwide), democracy, law and justice, economic prosperity and social security, and guarantee them for the future. Unemployment, inadequate growth and environmental pollution have long ceased to be merely national problems, and they cannot be solved at national level. It is only in the context of the EU that a stable economic order can be established and only through joint European efforts that we can secure an international economic policy that improves the performance of the European economy and contributes to social justice. Without internal cohesion, Europe cannot assert its political and economic independence from the rest of the world, win back its influence on the international stage and regain its role in world politics.

Unity can endure only where equality is the rule. No citizen of the Union may be placed at a disadvantage or discriminated against because of his or her nationality. Discriminatory treatment on the grounds of gender, race, ethnic origin, religion or beliefs, disability, age or sexual orientation must be combated. The Charter of Fundamental Rights of the European Union goes still further. Any discrimination based on any ground such as colour, genetic features, language, political or any other opinion, membership of a national minority, property or birth is prohibited. In addition, all Union citizens are equal before the law. As far as the Member States are concerned, the principle of equality means that no State has precedence over another, and natural differences such as size, population and differing structures must be addressed only in accordance with the principle of equality.

THE FUNDAMENTAL FREEDOMS

Freedom results directly from peace, unity and equality. Creating a larger entity by linking 27 States affords at the same time freedom of movement beyond national frontiers. This means, in particular, freedom of movement for workers, freedom of establishment, freedom to provide services, free movement of goods and free movement of capital. These fundamental freedoms guarantee business people freedom of decision-making, workers freedom to choose their place of work and consumers freedom of choice between the greatest possible variety of products. Freedom of competition permits businesses to offer their goods and services to an incomparably wider circle of potential customers. Workers can seek employment and change job according to their own wishes and interests throughout the entire territory of the EU. Consumers can select the cheapest and best products from the far greater range of goods on offer that results from increased competition.

However, transitional rules still apply in some cases to citizens of the Member States which joined the EU on 1 May 2004 and 1 January 2007. The Accession Treaty contained exceptions in particular with regard to the free movement of workers, the freedom to provide services and the freedom of establishment. As a result, the 'old' EU Member States can restrict the free movement of workers who are nationals of the 'new' Member States for a period of up to seven years by making access to employment subject to national or bilateral law.

THE PRINCIPLE OF SOLIDARITY

Solidarity is the necessary corrective to freedom, for inconsiderate exercise of freedom is always at the expense of others. For this reason, if a Community framework is to endure, it must also always recognise the solidarity of its members as a fundamental principle, and share both the advantages, i.e. prosperity, and the burdens equally and fairly among its members.

1 to 3 June 1955, Taormina (Italy).
Joseph Bech, Paul-Henri Spaak and Johan Willem Beyen in the garden
of the hotel where they were staying during the Messina Conference.
These three Foreign Affairs Ministers drew up the Benelux Memorandum
which was discussed by the Six during this conference.

RESPECT OF NATIONAL IDENTITY

The national identities of the Member States are respected. The idea is not for the Member States to be 'dissolved' into the EU, but rather for them to contribute their own particular qualities. It is precisely this variety of national characteristics and identities that lends the EU its moral authority, which in turn is used for the benefit of the EU as a whole.

THE NEED FOR SECURITY

All of these fundamental values are ultimately dependent on security. Particularly since the attack on the USA of 11 September 2001, the fight against terrorism and organised crime in Europe has also been in the spotlight again. Police and judicial cooperation continues to be consolidated, and protection of the EU's external borders intensified.

However, security in the European context also means the social security of all citizens living in the EU, job security and secure general economic and business conditions. In this respect, the EU institutions are called upon to make it possible for citizens and businesses to work out their future by creating the conditions on which they depend.

THE FUNDAMENTAL RIGHTS

The fundamental values and concepts at the heart of the EU also include the fundamental rights of individual citizens of the Union. The history of Europe has for more than 200 years been characterised by continuing efforts to enhance the protection of fundamental rights. Starting with the declarations of human and civil rights in the 18th century, fundamental rights and civil liberties have now become firmly anchored in the constitutions of most civilised states. This is especially true of the EU Member States, whose legal systems are constructed on the basis of the rule of law and respect for the dignity, freedom and the right to self-development of the individual. There are also numerous international conventions on the protection of human rights, among which the European Convention on Human Rights is of very great significance.

It was not until 1969 that the Court of Justice established a body of case-law to serve as a framework of fundamental rights. This was because in the early years the Court had rejected all actions relating to basic rights on the grounds that it need not concern itself with matters falling within the scope of national constitutional law. The Court had to alter its position not least because it was itself the embodiment of the primacy of Union law and its precedence over national law; this primacy can only be firmly established if Union law is sufficient in itself to guarantee the protection of basic rights with the same legal force as under the national constitutions.

The starting point in this case-law was the *Stauder* judgment, in which the point at issue was the fact that a recipient of welfare benefits for war victims regarded the requirement that he give his name when registering for the purchase of butter at reduced prices at Christmas time as a violation of his human dignity and the principle of equality. Although the Court of Justice came to the conclusion, in interpreting the Community provision, that it was not necessary for recipients to give their name so that, in fact, consideration of the question of a violation of a fundamental right was superfluous, it declared finally that the general fundamental principles of the Community legal order, which the Court of Justice had to safeguard, included respect for fundamental rights. This was the first time that the Court of Justice recognised the existence of an EU framework of fundamental rights of its own.

Initially, the Court developed its safeguards for fundamental rights from a number of provisions in the Treaties. This is especially the case for the numerous bans on discrimination which, in specific circumstances, address particular aspects of the general principle of equality. Examples are the prohibition of any discrimination on grounds of nationality (Article 18 TFEU), preventing people being treated differently on the grounds of gender, race, ethnic origin, religion or beliefs, disability, age or sexual orientation (Article 10 TFEU), the equal treatment of goods and persons in relation to the four basic freedoms (freedom of movement of goods — Article 34 TFEU; freedom of movement of persons — Article 45 TFEU; the right of establishment — Article 49 TFEU; and freedom to provide services — Article 57 TFEU), freedom of competition (Article 101 et seq. TFEU) and equal pay for men and women (Article 157 TFEU). The four fundamental freedoms of the Community, which guarantee the basic freedoms of professional life, can also be regarded as a Community fundamental right to freedom of movement and freedom to choose and practise a profession. Explicit guarantees are also provided for the right of association (Article 153 TFEU), the right to petition (Article 24 TFEU) and the protection of business and professional secrecy (Article 339 TFEU).

The Court of Justice has steadily developed and added to these initial attempts at protecting fundamental rights through Community law. It has done this by recognising and applying general legal principles, drawing on the concepts that are common to the constitutions of the Member States and on the international conventions on the protection of human rights to whose conclusion the Member States have been party. Prominent among the latter is the European Convention on Human Rights, which helped to shape the substance of fundamental rights in the Union and the mechanisms for their protection. On this basis, the Court has recognised a number of freedoms as basic rights secured by Community law: right of ownership, freedom to engage in an occupation, the inviolability of the home, freedom of opinion, general rights of personality, the protection of the family (e.g. family members' rights to join a migrant worker), economic freedom, freedom of religion or faith, as well as a number of fundamental procedural rights such as the right to due legal process, the principle of confidentiality of correspondence between lawyer and client (known as 'privileged communications' in the common-law countries), the ban on being punished twice for the same offence, or the requirement to provide justification for an EU legal act.

One particularly important principle regularly invoked in legal disputes is the principle of equal treatment. Put simply, this means that like cases must be treated alike, unless there is some objectively justifiable ground for distinguishing them. But the Court of Justice has held, contrary to international custom, that this principle does not preclude nationals and home-produced goods from being subjected to stricter requirements than citizens or products from other Member States. This 'reverse discrimination' is the inevitable result of the limited scope of the Union's powers and cannot be remedied by Community law. Under the Court's judgments issued up to now, the rules requiring liberalisation, which flow from the fundamental freedoms, apply only to cross-border trade. Rules regulating the production and marketing of home-produced goods or the legal status of nationals in their own Member State are affected by Community law only if the Union has introduced harmonisation measures.

The jurisprudence of the Court of Justice has given the Union an extensive body of quasi-constitutional law. In practical terms, the principle of proportionality is foremost among these. What it means is that the objectives pursued and the means deployed must be weighed up and an attempt made to keep them in proper balance so that the citizen is not subjected to excessive burdens. Among the other fundamental principles underlying Union law are the general principles of administrative law and the concept of due process: legitimate expectations must be protected, retroactive provisions imposing burdens or withdrawing legitimately acquired advantages are precluded and the right to due legal process — natural justice is the traditional term for this — must be secured in the administrative procedures of the Commission and the judicial procedures of the Court of Justice. Particular value is also attached to greater transparency, which means that decisions should be taken as openly as possible, and as closely as possible to the citizen. An important aspect of this transparency is that any EU citizen or legal person registered in a Member State may have access to Council or Commission documents. All grants and subsidies from the EU budget must also be disclosed to natural or legal persons by means of databases accessible to every Union citizen.

With all due respect for the achievements of the Court of Justice in the development of unwritten fundamental rights, this process of deriving 'European fundamental rights' had a serious disadvantage: the Court of Justice was confined to the particular case in point. It was therefore unable to develop fundamental rights from the general legal principles for all areas in which this appeared necessary or desirable. Nor was it able to elaborate the scope of and the limits to the protection of fundamental rights as generally and distinctively as was necessary. As a result, the EU institutions could not assess with enough precision whether they were in danger of violating a fundamental right or not. Nor could any Union citizen who was affected judge without further effort in every case whether one of his or her fundamental rights had been infringed.

For a long time, EU accession to the European Convention on Human Rights was regarded as a way out of this situation. In its Opinion 2/94, however, the Court held that, as the law stood, the EU had no competence to accede to the convention. The Court stated that respect for human rights was a condition for the lawfulness of EU acts. However, accession to the convention would entail a substantial change in the present Union system for the protection of human rights in that it would involve the EU entering into a distinct international institutional system as well as integration of all the provisions of the convention into the Union legal order. The Court took the view that such a modification of the system for the protection of human rights in the EU, with equally fundamental institutional implications for the Union and for the Member States, would be of constitutional significance and would therefore go beyond the scope of the dispositive powers provided for in Article 352 TFEU. The EU's accession to the convention was therefore specifically provided for in Article 6(2) of the EU Treaty. However, the Treaty of Lisbon made a further, decisive step towards the creation of a common constitutional law for the EU and put the protection of fundamental rights in the EU on a new footing. The new article on fundamental rights in the EU Treaty (Article 6 TEU) refers to the European Union's Charter of Fundamental Rights, declaring it to be binding for the actions of the EU institutions and the Member States, insofar as they apply and implement Union law.

This Charter of Fundamental Rights is based on a draft previously drawn up by a convention of 16 representatives of the Heads of State or Government of the Member States and of the President of the European Commission, 16 Members of the European Parliament, and 30 members of national parliaments (two from each of the then Member States) under the chairmanship of Professor Roman Herzog, and was solemnly proclaimed to be the 'European Union's Charter of Fundamental Rights' by the Presidents of the European Parliament, the Council and the European Commission on 7 December 2000. During the negotiations on a European constitution, this Charter of Fundamental Rights was revised and made an integral part of the Treaty establishing a Constitution for Europe of 29 October 2004. Following the failure of the Treaty, the Charter of Fundamental Rights was again solemnly proclaimed as the 'European Union's Charter of Fundamental Rights', this time as a separate instrument, by the Presidents of the European Parliament, the Council and the European Commission on 12 December 2007 in Strasbourg. The EU Treaty refers to this version of the charter in binding form. This makes the Charter of Fundamental Rights legally binding and also establishes the applicability of fundamental rights in Union law. However, this does not apply to Poland and the United Kingdom. These two Member States were unable, or did not wish, to adopt the system of fundamental rights of the charter, as they were concerned that they would be obliged to surrender or at least change certain national positions concerning, for example, religious issues or the treatment of minorities. They are therefore not bound by the fundamental rights of the charter, but by the case-law of the Court of Justice, as previously.

The 'constitution' of the European Union

Every social organisation has a constitution. A constitution is the means by which the structure of a political system is defined, i.e. the relationship of the various parts to each other and to the whole is specified, the common objectives are defined and the rules for making binding decisions are laid down. The constitution of the EU, as an association of states to which quite specific tasks and functions have been allotted, must thus be able to answer the same questions as the constitution of a state.

In the Member States the body politic is shaped by two overriding principles: the rule of law and democracy. All the activities of the Union, if they are to be true to the fundamental requirements of law and democracy, must therefore have both legal and democratic legitimacy: the elements on which it is founded, its structure, its powers, the way it operates, the position of the Member States and their institutions, and the position of the citizen.

Following the failure of the Treaty establishing a Constitution for Europe of 29 October 2004, the EU 'constitution' is still not laid down in a comprehensive constitutional document, as it is in most of the constitutions of its Member States, but arises from the totality of rules and fundamental values by which those in authority perceive themselves to be bound. These rules are to be found partly in the European Treaties or in the legal instruments produced by the Union institutions, but they also rest partly on custom.

The legal nature of the EU

Any consideration of the legal nature of the EU must start by looking at its characteristic features. Although the EU's legal nature was set out in two precedent-setting judgments of the Court of Justice in 1963 and 1964 relating to the then European Economic Community, the judgments are still valid for the European Union in its current form.

VAN GEND & LOOS

In this legal dispute, the Dutch transport company Van Gend & Loos filed an action against the Netherlands customs authorities for imposing an import duty on a chemical product from Germany which was higher than duties on earlier imports. The company considered this an infringement of Article 12 of the EEC Treaty, which prohibits the introduction of new import duties or any increase in existing customs duties between the Member States. The court in the Netherlands then suspended the proceedings and referred the matter to the Court of Justice for clarification as regards the scope and legal implications of the abovementioned article of the Treaty establishing the EC.

The Court of Justice used this case as an opportunity to set out a number of observations of a fundamental nature concerning the legal nature of the EU. In its judgment, the Court stated that:

'The objective of the EEC Treaty, which is to establish a common market, the functioning of which is of direct concern to interested parties in the Community, implies that this Treaty is more than an agreement which merely creates mutual obligations between the contracting States. This view is confirmed by the preamble to the Treaty, which refers not only to governments but to peoples. It is also confirmed more specifically by the establishment of institutions endowed with sovereign rights, the exercise of which affects Member States and also their citizens ... The conclusion to be drawn from this is that the Community constitutes a new legal order of international law for the benefit of which the States have limited their sovereign rights, albeit within limited fields, and the subjects of which comprise not only Member States but also their nationals.'

COSTA v ENEL

Just a year later, the *Costa* v *ENEL* case gave the Court of Justice an opportunity to set out its position in more detail. The facts of this case were as follows. In 1962, Italy nationalised the production and distribution of electricity and transferred the assets of the electricity undertakings to the national electricity board, ENEL. As a shareholder of Edison Volt, one of the companies that was nationalised, Mr Costa considered that he had been deprived of his dividend and consequently refused to pay an electricity bill for ITL 1 926. In proceedings before the arbitration court in Milan, one of the arguments put forward by Mr Costa to justify his conduct was that the nationalising act infringed a number of provisions of the EEC Treaty. In order to be able to assess Mr Costa's submissions in his defence, the court requested the Court of Justice to interpret various aspects of the EEC Treaty. In its judgment, the Court of Justice stated the following in relation to the legal nature of the EEC:

'By contrast with ordinary international treaties, the EEC Treaty has created its own legal system which ... became an integral part of the legal systems of the Member States and which their courts are bound to apply. By creating a Community of unlimited duration, having its own institutions, its own personality, its own legal capacity and capacity of representation on the international plane and, more particularly, real powers stemming from a limitation of sovereignty or a transfer of powers from the States to the Community, the Member States have limited their sovereign rights ... and have thus created a body of law which binds both their nationals and themselves.'

On the basis of its detailed observations, the Court reached the following conclusion:

'It follows from all these observations that the law stemming from the Treaty, an independent source of law, could not, because of its special and original nature, be overridden by domestic legal provisions, however framed, without being deprived of its character as Community law and without the legal basis of the Community itself being called into question. The transfer by the States from their domestic legal system to the Community legal system of the rights and obligations arising under the Treaty carries with it a permanent limitation of their sovereign rights, against which a subsequent unilateral act incompatible with the concept of the Community cannot prevail.'

In the light of these judgments, the elements which together typically characterise the special legal nature of the EU are:

- the institutional set-up, which ensures that action by the EU is also characterised by the overall European interest, i.e. is reflected in or influenced by the Union interest as laid down in the objectives;

- the transfer of powers to the Union institutions to a greater degree than in other international organisations, and extending to areas in which States normally retain their sovereign rights;

- the establishment of its own legal order which is independent of the Member States' legal orders;

- the direct applicability of Union law, which makes provisions of Union law fully and uniformly applicable in all Member States, and bestows rights and imposes obligations on both the Member States and their citizens;

- the primacy of Union law, which ensures that Union law may not be revoked or amended by national law and that it takes precedence over national law if the two conflict.

The EU is thus an autonomous entity with its own sovereign rights and a legal order independent of the Member States, to which both the Member States themselves and their nationals are subject within the EU's areas of competence.

The EU has, by its very nature, certain features in common with the usual kind of international organisation or federal-type structure, as well as a number of differences.

The EU is itself not yet a 'finished product'; it is in the process of evolving and the form it finally takes still cannot be predicted.

The only feature that the EU has in common with the traditional international organisations is that it too came into being as a result of an international treaty. However, the EU has already moved a long way from these beginnings. This is because, although the Treaties establishing the EU were based on international treaties, they led to the creation of an independent Union with its own sovereign rights and responsibilities. The Member States have ceded some of their sovereign powers to this Union. In addition, the tasks which have been allotted to the EU are very different from those of other international organisations. While the latter mainly have clearly defined tasks of a technical nature, the EU has areas of responsibility which together constitute essential attributes of statehood.

Through these differences between the EU and the traditional type of international organisation, the EU is in the process of acquiring a status similar to that of an individual state. In particular, the Member States' partial surrender of sovereign rights was taken as a sign that the EU was already structured along the lines of a federal state. However, this view fails to take into account that the EU institutions only have powers in certain areas to pursue the objectives specified in the Treaties. This means that they are not free to choose their objectives in the same way as a sovereign state; nor are they in a position to meet the challenges facing modern states today. The EU has neither the comprehensive jurisdiction enjoyed by sovereign states nor the powers to establish new areas of responsibility ('jurisdiction over jurisdiction').

The EU is therefore neither an international organisation in the usual sense nor an association of states, but rather an autonomous entity somewhere in between the two. In legal circles, the term 'supranational organisation' is now used.

THE TASKS OF THE **EU**

The list of tasks entrusted to the EU strongly resembles the constitutional order of a state. These are not the narrowly circumscribed technical tasks commonly assumed by international organisations, but fields of competence which, taken as a whole, form essential attributes of statehood.

The list of tasks entrusted to the EU is very wide-ranging, covering economic, social and political action.

The economic tasks are centred around establishing a common market that unites the national markets of the Member States and on which all goods and services can be offered and sold on the same conditions as on an internal market and to which all Union citizens have the same, free access.

The plan to create a common market has essentially been fulfilled through the programme aimed at completion of the internal market by 1992, which was initiated by the then President of the Commission, Jacques Delors, and approved by the Heads of State or Government, with the Union institutions succeeding in laying down a legal framework for a properly functioning single market. This framework has now been fleshed out very largely by national transposition measures, with the result that the single market has already become a reality. This single market also makes itself felt in everyday life, especially when travelling within the EU, where identity checks at national borders have long since been discontinued.

The internal market is backed up by the economic and monetary union.

The EU's task in economic policy is not, however, to lay down and operate a European economic policy, but to coordinate the national economic policies so that the policy decisions of one or more Member States do not have negative repercussions for the operation of the single market. To this end, a Stability and Growth Pact was adopted to give Member States the detailed criteria which their decisions on budgetary policy have to meet. If they fail to do this, the European Commission can issue warnings and, in cases of continuing excessive budgetary deficit, the Council can also impose penalties.

The EU's task in monetary policy was and is to introduce a single currency in the EU and to control monetary issues centrally. Some success has already been achieved in this area. On 1 January 1999, the euro was introduced as the single European currency in the Member States which had already met the convergence criteria established for that purpose. These were Belgium, Germany, Ireland, Spain, France, Italy, Luxembourg, the Netherlands, Austria, Portugal and Finland. On 1 January 2002 the national currencies of these States were replaced with euro bank notes and coins. Since then, their day-to-day payments and financial transactions have been made in only one currency — the euro. Greece and Sweden had, initially, failed to meet the convergence criteria. Greece was included on 1 January 2001. Sweden, which could not meet the criteria principally due to the fact that it did not participate in the exchange rate mechanism of the European Monetary System (the 'waiting room' for the euro), is subject to a derogation in that the Commission and the European Central Bank must present convergence reports for Sweden at least every two years, in which they can recommend Sweden's participation to the Council. If such a recommendation is made and approved by the Council, Sweden will not be able to refuse to participate. However, there is currently little support amongst the Swedish population for joining the euro area. In a 2003 referendum, 55.9 % were against the introduction of the euro. In a survey in December 2005, 49 % were still against the euro, while 36 % were in favour. The situation is different with regard to Denmark and the United Kingdom. These Member States secured an opt-out, which allows them to decide if and when the procedure for verifying compliance with the criteria for joining the single currency

6 December 1977, Brussels.
Demonstration in favour of elections based on
universal suffrage for the European Parliament
and of the single currency during the European
Council meeting on 5 and 6 December 1977.

is initiated. The new Member States are also obliged to adopt the euro as their national currency as soon as they meet the convergence criteria. None of the new Member States has an opt-out clause, and most of the new Member States wish to introduce the euro as soon as possible. Slovenia (1 January 2007), Cyprus (1 January 2008), Malta (1 January 2008) and Slovakia (1 January 2009) have already achieved this, extending the 'euro area' — countries which have the euro as their currency — to a current total of 16 Member States.

In addition to the area of economic and monetary policy, there are many other economic policy areas in which the EU has responsibilities. These include in particular agricultural and fisheries policy, transport policy, consumer policy, structural and cohesion policy, research and development policy, space policy, environment policy, health policy, trade policy and energy policy.

In social policy the EU has the task of ensuring that the benefits of economic integration are not only felt by those active in the economy, but also shape the social dimension of the single market. One of the starting points for this has been the introduction of a social security system for migrant workers. Under this system, workers who have worked in more than one Member State, and therefore fallen under different social insurance schemes, will not suffer a disadvantage with regard to their social security (old-age pension, invalidity pension, health care, family benefits, unemployment benefits). A further priority task of social policy, in view of the unemployment situation in the EU, which has been a source of concern for a number of years, has been the need to devise a European employment strategy. This calls on the Member States and the EU to develop a strategy for employment and particularly to promote a skilled, trained and adaptable workforce, in addition to which labour markets should also be made adaptable to economic change. Employment promotion is regarded as a matter of common concern, and requires Member States to coordinate their national measures within the Council. The EU will contribute to a high level of employment by encouraging cooperation between Member States and, if necessary, complementing their action while respecting their competences.

With regard to the actual area of politics, the EU has tasks in the areas of Union citizenship, policy on judicial cooperation in criminal matters and common foreign and security policy. Union citizenship has further strengthened the rights and interests of nationals of the Member States within the EU. Citizens enjoy the right to move freely within the Union (Article 21 TFEU), the right to vote and stand as a candidate in local elections (Article 22

TFEU), entitlement to protection by the diplomatic and consular authorities of any Member State (Article 23 TFEU), the right to petition the European Parliament (Article 24 TFEU) and, in the context of the general ban on discrimination, the right to be treated by all Member States in the same way as they treat their own nationals (Article 20(2) in conjunction with Article 18 TFEU). With respect to common foreign and security policy, the EU has, in particular, the tasks of:

- safeguarding the commonly held values, fundamental interests and independence of the EU;

- strengthening the security of the EU and its Member States;

- securing world peace and increasing international security;

- promoting international cooperation;

- promoting democracy and the rule of law, and safeguarding human rights and basic freedoms;

- establishing a common defence.

Since the EU is not an individual state, these tasks can only be carried out step by step. Traditionally, foreign and especially security policy are areas in which the Member States are particularly keen to retain their own (national) sovereignty. Another reason why common interests in this area are difficult to define is that only France and the United Kingdom have nuclear weapons. Another problem is that some Member States are not in NATO or the WEU. Most 'common foreign and security policy' decisions are therefore still currently taken on the basis of cooperation between states. In the meantime, however, a range of tools has emerged in its own right, thus giving cooperation between states a firm legal framework.

In the area of judicial cooperation in criminal matters, the main role of the EU is to carry out tasks that are in the interests of Europe as a whole. These include, in particular, combating organised crime, preventing trafficking in human beings and prosecuting criminal offences. Since organised crime can no longer be effectively countered at national level, a joint response at EU level is needed. Two very positive steps have already been taken with the directive on money-laundering and the creation of a European police authority, Europol, which has been operational since 1998 (Article 88 TFEU). This cooperation is also concerned with facilitating and accelerating cooperation in relation to proceedings and the enforcement of decisions, facilitating extradition between Member States, establishing minimum rules relating to the constituent elements of criminal acts and to penalties in the fields of organised crime, terrorism, trafficking in human beings and the sexual exploitation of women and children, illicit drug trafficking and illicit arms trafficking, money-laundering and corruption (Article 83 TFEU). One of the most significant advances in EU judicial cooperation was the creation of Eurojust in April 2003 (Article 85 TFEU). Based in The Hague, Eurojust is a team of magistrates and prosecutors from all EU countries. Its job is to help coordinate the investigation and prosecution of serious cross-border crimes. From Eurojust the Council may establish a European Public Prosecutor's Office in order to combat crimes affecting the financial interests of the Union (Article 86 TFEU). Further progress has been made with the European arrest warrant, which has been valid throughout the EU since January 2004. The warrant can be issued for anyone accused of an offence for which the minimum penalty is more than one year in prison. The European arrest warrant is designed to replace lengthy extradition procedures.

THE POWERS OF THE EU

The Treaties establishing the EU do not confer on the Union institutions any general power to take all measures necessary to achieve the objectives of the Treaty, but lay down in each chapter the extent of the powers to act. As a basic principle, the EU and its institutions do not have the power to decide on their legal basis and competencies; the principle of specific conferment of powers (Article 2 TFEU) continues to apply. This method has been chosen by the Member States in order to ensure that the surrender of their own powers can be more easily monitored and controlled.

The range of matters covered by the specific conferment of powers varies according to the nature of the tasks allotted to the EU. Competences which have not been transferred to the EU remain in the exclusive power of the Member States. The EU Treaty explicitly states that matters of national security stay under the exclusive authority of the Member States.

This naturally begs the question of where the dividing line is between EU competences and those of the Member States. This dividing line is drawn on the basis of three categories of competence:

■ exclusive competence of the EU (Article 3 TFEU) in areas where it can be assumed that a measure at EU level will be more effective than a measure in any Member State that is not coordinated. These areas are clearly set out and comprise the customs union, the establishing of the competition rules necessary for the functioning of the internal market, the monetary policy of the euro States, the common commercial policy and parts of the common fisheries policy. In these policy areas only the European Union may legislate and adopt legally binding acts, the Member States being able to do so themselves only if so empowered by the European Union or for the implementation of Union acts (Article 2(1) TFEU);

■ shared competence between the EU and the Member States (Article 4 TFEU) in areas where action at European level will add value over action by Member States. There is shared competence for internal market rules, economic, social and territorial cohesion, agriculture and fisheries, environment, transport, trans-European networks, energy supply and the area of freedom, security and justice, and also for common safety concerns in public health matters, research and technological development, space, development cooperation and humanitarian aid. In all these areas the EU can exercise competence first, but only with regard to matters laid down in the relevant Union instrument, and not to the entire policy area. The Member States exercise their competence to the extent that the EU has not exercised, or has decided to cease exercising, its competence (Article 2(2) TFEU). The latter situation arises when the relevant EU institutions decide to repeal a legislative act, in particular to respect the principles of subsidiarity and proportionality. The Council may, on the initiative of one or more of its members, request that the Commission submit proposals for repealing a legislative act;

■ competence to carry out supporting action (Article 6 TFEU). The EU's competence to carry out supporting action is limited to coordinating or providing complementary action for the action of the Member States; the EU cannot harmonise national law in the areas concerned (Article 2(5) TFEU). Responsibility for drafting legislation therefore continues to lie with the Member States, which thus have considerable freedom to act. The areas covered by this category of competence are protection and improvement of human health, industry, culture, tourism, education, youth, sport and vocational training, civil protection and administrative cooperation. In the areas of employment and economic policy, the Member States explicitly acknowledge the need to coordinate national measures within the EU.

It should be noted that the EU's competences in the area of coordination of economic and employment policy and in the area of common foreign and security policy do not fall under any of these three categories, and therefore do not belong to this set of competences. However, a declaration is made stating that the EU's common foreign and security policy will not affect the Member States' competence for their own foreign policy and national standing in the world. In addition to these special powers to act, the Union Treaties also confer on the institutions a power to act when it is essential for the operation of the single market or for ensuring undistorted competition (see Article 352 TFEU — dispositive powers or flexibility clause). These articles do not, however, confer on the institutions any general power enabling them to carry out tasks which lie outside the objectives laid down in the Treaties, and the Union institutions cannot extend their powers to the detriment of those of the Member States. In practice, the possibilities afforded by this power were used very often in the past, since the EU was over time faced repeatedly with new tasks that were not foreseen at the time the founding Treaties were concluded, and for which accordingly no appropriate powers were conferred in the Treaties. Examples are the protection of the environment and of consumers or the establishment of the European Regional Development Fund as a means of closing the gap between the developed and underdeveloped regions of the EU. Now, however, specific jurisdiction has been given in the abovementioned fields. These specific provisions have meant that the practical importance of the dispositive powers has very much declined.

The exercise of these powers requires the approval of the European Parliament. Finally, there are further powers to take such measures as are indispensable for the effective and meaningful implementation of powers that have already been expressly conferred (implied powers). These powers have acquired a special significance in the conduct of external relations. They enable the EU to assume obligations towards non-member countries or other international organisations in fields covered by the list of tasks entrusted to the EU. An outstanding example is provided by the Kramer case ruled on by the Court of Justice. This case concerned the EU's capacity to cooperate with international organisations in fixing fishing quotas and, where considered appropriate, to assume obligations on the matter under international law. Since there was no specific provision laid down in the Treaty, the Court inferred the necessary external competence of the EU from its internal competence for fisheries policy under the common agricultural policy.

However, in the exercise of these powers, the EU is governed by the subsidiarity principle, taken over from Roman Catholic social doctrine, which has acquired virtually constitutional status through being embodied in the EU Treaty (Article 5(3)). There are two facets to it: the affirmative statement that the EU must act where the objectives to be pursued can be better attained at the Union level, which enhances its powers; and the negative statement that it must not act where objectives can be satisfactorily attained by the Member States acting individually, which constrains them. What this means in practice is that all Union institutions, but especially the Commission, must always demonstrate that there is a real need for common rules and common action. To paraphrase Montesquieu, when it is not necessary for the EU to take action, it is necessary that it should take none. If the need for Union rules is demonstrated, the next question that arises concerns the intensity and the form that they should take. The answer flows from the principle of proportionality that has entered Union law through the decisions of the Court of Justice of the European Union, and is established in the EU Treaty in conjunction with the competence provisions (Article 5(4)). It means that the need for the specific legal instrument must be thoroughly assessed to see whether there is a less constraining means of achieving the same result. The main conclusion to be reached in general terms is that framework legislation, minimum standards and mutual recognition of the Member States' existing standards should always be preferred to excessively detailed legal provisions.

National parliaments can also now check compliance with the principles of subsidiarity and proportionality. For this purpose, an early warning system has been introduced, allowing national parliaments to issue a reasoned position within eight weeks following transmission of the legislative proposal, setting out why the legislative proposal in question does not meet the subsidiarity and proportionality requirements. If this reasoned position is supported by at least a third of the votes allocated to the national parliaments (where each national parliament has two votes, or, in the case of chamber systems, one vote per chamber), the legislative proposal must be reviewed again by the institution that issued it (usually the Commission). Following this review, the proposal can be retained, amended or withdrawn. If the European Commission decides to retain the draft, it must issue a reasoned opinion, stating why it considers the draft to follow the subsidiarity principle. This reasoned opinion is sent to the EU legislator together with the reasoned opinions of the national parliaments so that they can be taken into account in the legislative procedure. If, by a 55 % majority of the Members of the Council of the EU or by a majority of the votes cast in the European Parliament, the EU legislator is of the opinion that the proposal does not comply with the subsidiarity principle, the legislative proposal is not examined any further.

THE INSTITUTIONS OF THE **EU**

Article 13 of the TEU (institutional framework)

1. The Union shall have an institutional framework which shall aim to promote its values, advance its objectives, serve its interests, those of its citizens and those of the Member States, and ensure the consistency, effectiveness and continuity of its policies and actions.

The Union's institutions shall be:

— the European Parliament,
— the European Council,
— the Council,
— the European Commission (hereinafter referred to as 'the Commission'),
— the Court of Justice of the European Union,
— the European Central Bank,
— the Court of Auditors.

2. Each institution shall act within the limits of the powers conferred on it in the Treaties, and in conformity with the procedures, conditions and objectives set out in them. The institutions shall practise mutual sincere cooperation.

3. The provisions relating to the European Central Bank and the Court of Auditors and detailed provisions on the other institutions are set out in the Treaty on the Functioning of the European Union.

4. The European Parliament, the Council and the Commission shall be assisted by an Economic and Social Committee and a Committee of the Regions acting in an advisory capacity.

OVERVIEW OF THE EU INSTITUTIONS, ACCORDING TO THE TFEU

EUROPEAN COUNCIL
27 Heads of State or Government, President of the European
Council and President of the Commission

COUNCIL
27 Ministers
(one per Member State)

**EUROPEAN
PARLIAMENT**
751 Members ([2])

EUROPEAN COMMISSION
27 Members (until 2014)

**COMMITTEE OF
THE REGIONS**
350 Members (maximum)

**EUROPEAN ECONOMIC AND
SOCIAL COMMITTEE**
350 Members (maximum)

**COURT OF JUSTICE OF THE
EUROPEAN UNION**

**EUROPEAN
CENTRAL
BANK**

**COURT OF
AUDITORS**
27 Members
(one per
Member State)

**EUROPEAN
INVESTMENT
BANK**

([2]) *When the Lisbon Treaty came into force on 1 December 2009, the number of
Members was increased temporarily to 754. However, the maximum of 751
must be restored by the next elections of 2014.*

MEMBER STATE	VOTES IN THE COUNCIL	SEATS IN THE EUROPEAN PARLIAMENT
GERMANY	29	99
FRANCE	29	78
ITALY	29	78
UNITED KINGDOM	29	78
SPAIN	27	54
POLAND	27	54
ROMANIA	14	35
NETHERLANDS	13	27
BELGIUM	12	24
CZECH REPUBLIC	12	24
GREECE	12	24
HUNGARY	12	24
PORTUGAL	12	24
SWEDEN	10	19
BULGARIA	10	18
AUSTRIA	10	18
DENMARK	7	14
SLOVAKIA	7	14
FINLAND	7	14
IRELAND	7	13
LITHUANIA	7	13
LATVIA	4	9
SLOVENIA	4	7
ESTONIA	4	6
CYPRUS	4	6
LUXEMBOURG	4	6
MALTA	3	5

Another question arising in connection with the constitution of the European Union is that of its organisation. What are the institutions of the Union? Since the EU exercises functions normally reserved for States, does it have a government, a parliament, administrative authorities and courts like those with which we are familiar in the Member States? Action on the tasks assigned to the EU and the direction of the integration process was intentionally not left to Member States or to international cooperation. The EU has an institutional system that equips it to give new stimuli and objectives to the unification of Europe and to create a body of law that is uniformly devised and binding in all the Member States in the matters falling within its responsibility.

The main players in the EU institutional system are the EU institutions — the European Parliament, the European Council, the Council, the European Commission, the Court of Justice of the European Union, the European Central Bank and Court of Auditors. The ancillary bodies in the institutional system of the EU are the European Investment Bank, the European Economic and Social Committee and the Committee of the Regions.

THE INSTITUTIONS

The European Parliament (Article 14 TEU)

The European Parliament represents the peoples of the EU Member States. It is an amalgamation of the ECSC Joint Assembly, the EEC Assembly and the Euratom Assembly, which were combined to form an 'assembly' under the 1957 Convention on Certain Institutions Common to the European Communities ('first merger Treaty'). The name was not officially changed to 'European Parliament' until the EC Treaty was amended by the Treaty on European Union, although this step merely reflected what was already common usage dating back to the Assembly's own change of its name to 'European Parliament' in 1958.

Composition and election

Since the entry into force of the Lisbon Treaty on 1 December 2009, the European Parliament has had 754 seats. This exceeds the maximum of 751 Members laid down in the TEU (Article 14(2)), but must be accepted for the 2009–14 legislative period, as the MEPs elected in June cannot lose their seats. However, the maximum number of Members must be adhered to at the next elections in 2014. These are allocated to the Member States so that although each Member from a highly populated Member State represents more citizens than every Member from a State with a low population, no State with a lower population has more seats than a State with a higher population. As a general rule, the minimum number of seats per Member State is six, and the maximum 96, but, owing to the late entry into force of the Lisbon Treaty, an exception has been made for Germany in the 2009–14 legislative period, permitting it to continue to have 99 Members (MEPs elected in June 2009 cannot lose their seats because of the entry into force of the Lisbon Treaty) .

The exact composition has yet to be determined by the Council. This should have been done in time for the direct elections to the European Parliament in June 2009. However, since the Lisbon Treaty did not enter into force before the elections in June 2009, the new rules on the composition of the European Parliament could not be applied to the 2009–14 legislative period. Instead, the distribution of seats resulting from the accession of Bulgaria and Romania applied for these elections to the European Parliament. Upon the entry into force of the Lisbon Treaty on 1 December 2009, the number of Members rose by 18 to 754, with the new Members coming from 12 different Member States.

The composition of the European Parliament is shown in graphic form below; this is the situation in the current 2009–14 legislative period. The changes brought about by the Lisbon Treaty are indicated.

PRESIDENT
14 Vice-Presidents
5 Quaestors (advisory)

The President, Vice-Presidents and Quaestors make up the Bureau, which is elected by Parliament for terms of two and a half years. Another body, the Conference of Presidents, also includes the chairs of the political groups. It is responsible for the organisation of Parliament's work, and relations with the other EU institutions and with non-Union institutions.

PARLIAMENT PLENARY SESSION WITH 754 MEMBERS

MEMBER STATE	SEATS IN THE EUROPEAN PARLIAMENT
GERMANY	99
FRANCE	72 + 2
ITALY	72 + 1
UNITED KINGDOM	72 + 1
SPAIN	50 + 4
POLAND	50 + 1
ROMANIA	33
NETHERLANDS	25 + 1
BELGIUM	22
CZECH REPUBLIC	22
GREECE	22
HUNGARY	22
PORTUGAL	22
SWEDEN	18 + 2
BULGARIA	17 + 1
AUSTRIA	17 + 2
DENMARK	13
SLOVAKIA	13
FINLAND	13
IRELAND	12
LITHUANIA	12
LATVIA	8 + 1
SLOVENIA	7 + 1
ESTONIA	6
CYPRUS	6
LUXEMBOURG	6
MALTA	5 + 1

Up to 1979, representatives in the European Parliament were selected from the membership of national parliaments and delegated by them to the European Parliament. The direct general election of MEPs by the peoples of the Member States was provided for in the Treaties themselves, but the first direct elections were not held until June 1979, a number of earlier initiatives having been fruitless. Elections are now held every five years, which corresponds to the length of a 'legislative period'. Following decades of efforts, a uniform electoral procedure was finally introduced by the act concerning the election of representatives of the European Parliament by direct universal suffrage of 20 September 1976, as last amended by Council decision of 25 June and 23 September 2002 (known as the Direct Elections Act). Under this act, each Member State lays down its own election procedure, but must apply the same basic democratic rules: direct general election, proportional representation, free and secret ballots, minimum age (for the right to vote, this is 18 in all Member States except Austria, where the voting age was reduced to 16), renewable five-year term of office, incompatibilities (MEPs may not hold two offices at the same time, e.g. the office of judge, public prosecutor, Minister; they are also subject to the laws of their country, which may further limit their ability to hold more than one post or office), election date and equality between men and women. In some countries (Belgium, Greece and Luxembourg), voting is compulsory. In addition, a statute for Members of the European Parliament came into force on 14 July 2009. This new statute makes the terms and conditions of MEPs' work more transparent and contains clear rules. It also introduces a uniform salary for all MEPs, which is paid from the EU budget.

Now that it is directly elected, Parliament enjoys democratic legitimacy and can truly claim to represent the citizens of the EU Member States. But the mere existence of a directly elected Parliament cannot satisfy the fundamental requirement of a democratic constitution, which is that all public authority must emanate from the people. That does not only mean that the decision-making process must be transparent and the decision-making institutions representative; parliamentary control is required, and Parliament must lend legitimacy to the Union institutions involved in the decision-making process. A great deal of progress has been made in this area over recent years. Not only have the rights of Parliament been continually extended, but the Treaty of Lisbon has explicitly established the obligation for EU action to adhere to the principle of representative democracy. As a result, all citizens of the Union are directly represented in Parliament and entitled to participate actively in the EU's democratic life. The underlying objective of this is that decisions at EU level are taken as openly as possible and as closely as possible to the citizen. The political parties at EU level are to contribute to the shaping of a European identity and to articulate the will of the Union's citizens. If there is any deficit to the current democratic model of the EU, it is that the European Parliament, unlike the true parliaments in a parliamentary democracy, does not elect a government that answers to it.

Article 10 of the TEU (representative democracy)

1. The functioning of the Union shall be founded on representative democracy.

2. Citizens are directly represented at Union level in the European Parliament.

Member States are represented in the European Council by their Heads of State or Government and in the Council by their governments, themselves democratically accountable either to their national Parliaments, or to their citizens.

3. Every citizen shall have the right to participate in the democratic life of the Union. Decisions shall be taken as openly and as closely as possible to the citizen.

4. Political parties at European level contribute to forming European political awareness and to expressing the will of citizens of the Union.

However, the reason for this deficit is that, quite simply, no government in the normal sense exists at EU level. Instead, the functions analogous to government provided for in the Union Treaties are performed by the Council and the European Commission according to a form of division of labour. Nevertheless, the Treaty of Lisbon gave Parliament extensive powers in respect of appointments to the Commission, ranging from election by Parliament of the President of the Commission on the recommendation of the European Council, to Parliament's vote of approval of the full college of Commissioners ('right of investiture'). However, Parliament has no such influence over the membership of the Council, which is subject to parliamentary control only insofar as each of its members, as a national Minister, is answerable to the national parliament.

The role of the European Parliament in the EU's legislative process has increased considerably. The raising of the co-decision procedure to the level of ordinary legislative procedure has, in effect, turned the European Parliament into a 'co-legislator' alongside the Council.

In the ordinary legislative procedure, Parliament can not only put forward amendments to legislation at various readings but also, within certain limits, get them accepted by the Council. Union legislation cannot be passed without agreement between the Council and the European Parliament.

Traditionally, Parliament has also played a major role in the budgetary procedure. The Treaty of Lisbon further extended the budgetary powers of the European Parliament, stipulating that Parliament must approve the multiannual financial plan and giving it co-decision powers on all expenditure (compulsory and non-compulsory expenditure are no longer distinguished).

Parliament has a right of assent to all major international agreements concerning an area covered by co-decision, and to the Accession Treaties concluded with new Member States laying down the conditions of admission.

The supervisory powers of the European Parliament have also grown significantly over time. They are exercised mainly through the fact that the Commission must answer to Parliament, defend its proposals before it and present it with an annual report on the activities of the EU for debate. Parliament can, by a two-thirds majority of its members, pass a motion of censure and thereby compel the Commission to resign as a body (Article 234 TFEU). Several such motions have been put before the Parliament, but none has yet been even near achieving the required majority. The resignation of the Santer Commission in 1999 was triggered by Parliament's refusal to discharge it with regard to financial management; the motion of censure that had also been brought was unsuccessful, although only by small margin. Since in practice the Council also answers parliamentary questions, Parliament has the opportunity for direct political debate with two major institutions. These supervisory powers of Parliament have since been boosted. It is now also empowered to set up special Committees of Inquiry to look specifically at alleged cases of infringement of Community law or maladministration. A committee of this kind was used, for example, to look into the Commission's responsibility for the delay in responding to 'mad cow disease' in the United Kingdom, which also represented a threat to human life and health. Also written into the Treaties is the right of any natural or legal person to address petitions to Parliament, which are then dealt with by a standing Committee on Petitions. Finally, Parliament has also made use of its power to appoint an Ombudsman to whom complaints about maladministration in the activities of Union institutions or bodies, with the exception of the Court of Justice, can be referred. The Ombudsman may conduct enquiries and must inform the institution or body concerned of such action, and must submit to Parliament a report on the outcome of his or her inquiries.

Working procedures

The basic rules governing the workings of Parliament are set out in its rules of procedure.

The MEPs form political groups. Given Parliament's status as a Union institution, these are Union-wide party political groupings that cut across national lines.

Parliament holds its week-long plenary sessions in Strasbourg once a month, except in August. Additional sessions may also be held, particularly in connection with the budget. Shorter sessions (lasting one or two days) are held in Brussels. Lastly, emergency sessions may be convened to deal with current major issues, enabling Parliament to set out its position without delay on matters of importance (such as Union affairs, international affairs, violations of human rights). All plenary sessions are open to the public.

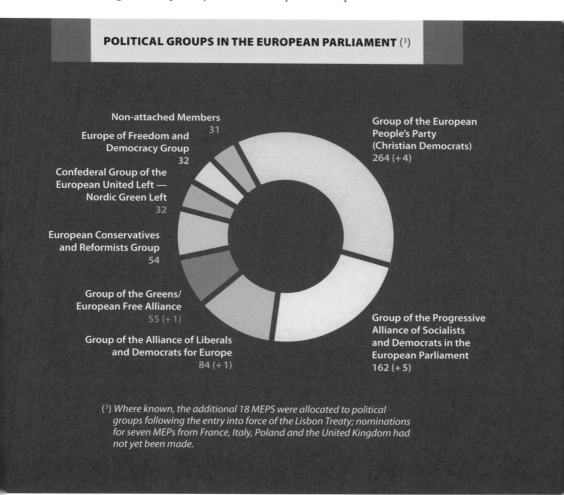

POLITICAL GROUPS IN THE EUROPEAN PARLIAMENT (³)

Non-attached Members
31

Europe of Freedom and
Democracy Group
32

Confederal Group of the
European United Left —
Nordic Green Left
32

European Conservatives
and Reformists Group
54

Group of the Greens/
European Free Alliance
55 (+1)

Group of the Alliance of Liberals
and Democrats for Europe
84 (+1)

Group of the European
People's Party
(Christian Democrats)
264 (+4)

Group of the Progressive
Alliance of Socialists
and Democrats in the
European Parliament
162 (+5)

(³) *Where known, the additional 18 MEPS were allocated to political groups following the entry into force of the Lisbon Treaty; nominations for seven MEPs from France, Italy, Poland and the United Kingdom had not yet been made.*

Decision-making procedures

An absolute majority of the votes cast is usually sufficient for a decision to be taken. As Parliament increases in importance, however, ever stricter requirements are imposed with regard to MEPs' attendance. A whole range of decisions may be adopted only if supported by an absolute majority of all Members of Parliament. Finally, any motion of censure against the European Commission must not only be backed by a majority of MEPs but also requires two thirds of the votes cast to be in favour.

PERMANENT COMMITTEES OF THE EUROPEAN PARLIAMENT
Foreign Affairs Committee (with 'Human Rights' and 'Security and Defence' subcommittees)
Development Committee
International Trade Committee
Budgets Committee
Budgetary Control Committee
Economic and Monetary Affairs Committee
Employment and Social Affairs Committee
Environment, Public Health and Food Safety Committee
Industry, Research and Energy Committee
Internal Market and Consumer Protection Committee
Transport and Tourism Committee
Regional Development Committee
Agriculture and Rural Development Committee
Fisheries Committee
Culture and Education Committee
Legal Affairs Committee
Civil Liberties, Justice and Home Affairs Committee
Constitutional Affairs Committee
Women's Rights and Gender Equality Committee
Petitions Committee

Seat

The European Council decided that Parliament's seat was to be in Strasbourg and thus ended the provisional status of an arrangement that had been in place for 30 years. It had become established practice for plenary sessions to be held in Strasbourg and Brussels, meetings of the political groups and committees to be held in Brussels during weeks when Parliament was not sitting, and for Parliament's Secretariat-General to be based in Luxembourg. The Council's decision on the location of the seats of the institutions confirmed the validity of these arrangements, subject to the proviso that the 12 periods of monthly plenary sessions should be held in Strasbourg. The unsatisfactory result of this decision is that MEPs and some Parliament officials and employees must commute between Strasbourg, Brussels and Luxembourg — a very costly business.

The European Council (Article 15 TEU)

The European Council grew out of the summit conferences of EU Heads of State or Government. At the Paris Summit in December 1974 it was decided that meetings should be held three times a year and described as the European Council. Since then, the European Council has become an independent body of the European Union (Article 13 TEU).

The Heads of State or Government and the President of the European Commission meet at least twice every half a year in this context. When the questions under discussion so demand, the Members of the European Council can decide to seek the support of a Minister and, in the case of the President of the Commission, of one Member of the European Commission to assist them in their work (Article 15(3) TEU).

The Treaty of Lisbon created the office of President of the European Council ([4]). The President of the European Council, unlike the Presidency up to now, has a European mandate, not a national one, running for two and a half years on a full-time basis. The person appointed President should be an outstanding personality, selected by qualified-majority voting of the Members of the European Council. Re-election is possible once. The President's tasks comprise the preparation and follow-up of European Council meetings and representing the EU at international summits in the area of foreign and security policy.

([4]) *Herman van Rompuy, at that time the Prime Minister of Belgium, was nominated as the first President of the European Council and took up office on 1 December 2009.*

The actual function of the European Council itself is to establish the general policy guidelines for EU action. It does so by taking basic policy decisions and issuing instructions and guidelines to the Council or the European Commission. The European Council has in this way directed work on economic and monetary union, the European Monetary System, direct elections to Parliament and a number of accession issues.

The Council (Article 16 TEU)

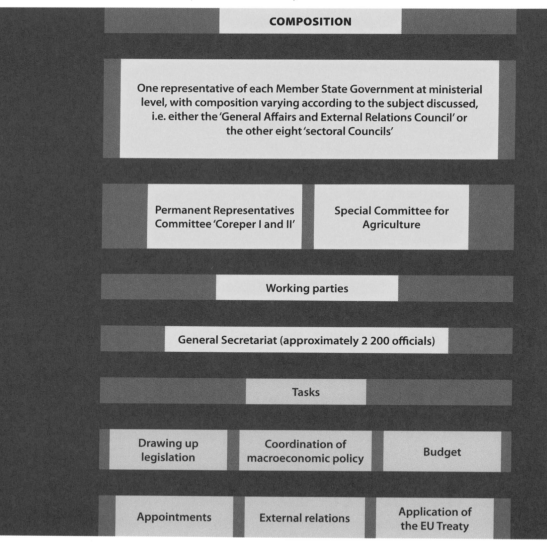

COMPOSITION

One representative of each Member State Government at ministerial level, with composition varying according to the subject discussed, i.e. either the 'General Affairs and External Relations Council' or the other eight 'sectoral Councils'

Permanent Representatives Committee 'Coreper I and II'

Special Committee for Agriculture

Working parties

General Secretariat (approximately 2 200 officials)

Tasks

Drawing up legislation

Coordination of macroeconomic policy

Budget

Appointments

External relations

Application of the EU Treaty

Composition and Presidency

The Council is made up of representatives of the governments of the Member States. All 27 Member States send one representative — as a rule, though not necessarily, the departmental or junior minister responsible for the matters under consideration. It is important that these representatives are empowered to act with binding effect on their governments. The very fact that governments may be represented in various ways obviously means that there are no permanent members of the Council; instead, the representatives sitting in the Council meet in nine different configurations depending on the subjects under discussion. These are: (1) 'General Affairs and External Relations Council': as the 'General Affairs Council', this Council coordinates the work of the Council in its various configurations and, together with the President of the European Council and the European Commission, prepares the European Council meetings; as the 'Foreign Affairs Council', it handles the EU's action abroad in accordance with the strategic guidelines of the European Council and ensures that the EU's action is consistent and coherent. The 'General Affairs and External Relations Council' is made up of the Foreign Ministers; its general affairs meetings are chaired by the ruling Presidency, and those on foreign affairs are chaired by the High Representative of the Union for Foreign Affairs and Security Policy. There are eight further Council formations attended by the Ministers from the Member States responsible for the areas concerned: (2) 'Economic and Financial Affairs' (commonly known as the Ecofin Council), (3) 'Cooperation in the fields of Justice and Home Affairs', (4) 'Employment, Social Policy, Health and Consumer Affairs', (5) 'Competitiveness', (6) 'Transport, Telecommunications and Energy', (7) 'Agriculture and Fisheries', (8) 'Environment' and (9) 'Education, Youth and Culture'.

The Presidency of the Council — with the exception of the Council of Foreign Ministers, which is chaired by the High Representative of the Union for Foreign Affairs and Security Policy— is held by each Member State in turn for six months. The order in which the office of President is held is decided unanimously by the Council. The Presidency changes hands on 1 January and 1 July each year (2008: Slovenia and France; 2009: the Czech Republic and Sweden; 2010: Spain and Belgium; 2011: Hungary and Poland; 2012: Denmark and Cyprus; 2013: Ireland and Lithuania, etc.). Given this fairly rapid 'turnover', each Presidency bases its action on a work programme agreed with the next two Presidencies and therefore valid for a

20 July 1979, Strasbourg.
Simone Veil becomes the President of
the first European Parliament, elected by
universal suffrage.

period of 18 months ('team Presidency'). The Presidency is mainly responsible for overall coordination of the work of the Council and the committees providing it with input. It is also important in political terms in that the Member State holding the EU Presidency enjoys an enhanced role on the world stage, and small Member States in particular are thus given an opportunity to rub shoulders with the 'major players' and make their mark in European politics.

The seat of the Council is in Brussels.

Tasks

The top priority of the Council is legislation, which it carries out together with Parliament in the co-decision process. The Council is also responsible for ensuring coordination of the economic policies of the Member States. It also establishes the budget on the basis of a preliminary draft from the Commission, although this must still be approved by Parliament. In addition, it issues a recommendation to Parliament on giving discharge to the Commission in respect of the implementation of the budget, and is responsible for appointing the members of the Court of Auditors, the European Economic and Social Committee and the Committee of the Regions. The Council is also is responsible for concluding agreements between the EU and non-member countries or international organisations.

Working procedures

The Council's working procedures are set out in detail in its rules of procedure. In practice, the Council's activities are basically made up of three stages, as follows.

Preparation for Council meetings

Preparatory work for Council meetings is carried out by two permanent bodies within its organisational structure: the Permanent Representatives Committee and the General Secretariat.

The Permanent Representatives Committee, which is referred to as Coreper, a contraction of its French title *Comité des représentants permanents*, prepares the ground for the Council's work and performs the tasks assigned to it by the Council. To enable it to carry out all these tasks, it is divided up into Coreper I (comprising the Deputy Permanent Representatives and primarily responsible for preparatory work on more technical matters dealt with by the various Councils) and Coreper II (comprising the Permanent Representatives themselves and basically responsible for all policy matters). Agriculture is the one area not subject to this division of tasks; a Special Committee on Agriculture (SCA, also known by its French abbreviation CSA — *Comité spécial de l'Agriculture*) was set up in 1960 and assumed Coreper's tasks on agricultural matters.

Preparations for Council meetings by Coreper and the SCA are of two kinds. Firstly, efforts are made to reach agreement at committee level, in connection with which the committees can draw on the assistance of around 100 permanent sector-specific working parties within the Council. They may also call on the services of 'ad hoc groups', which are assigned to deal with a particular problem within a specified period. Secondly, preparatory work must ensure that the issues to be discussed and decided on at Council meetings have been worked out in advance, and that the Council members are properly briefed. These dual approaches are reflected in the agenda of meetings: issues on which it was possible to reach agreement are referred to as 'A items' and those questions which are undecided and need to be discussed further are known as 'B items'.

The General Secretariat provides administrative assistance to the Council (and also to Coreper and the SCA). In particular, it handles the technical side of preparations for meetings of the Council, is in charge of providing interpretation facilities (the representatives of the Member States speak in their own language), ensures that any required translations are provided, provides legal advice to the Council and the committees, and administers the Council's budget.

Meetings of the Council

Meetings of the Council are convened by its President (the representative of the Member State holding the Presidency of the Council or the High Representative of the Union for Foreign Affairs and Security Policy) on his or her own initiative, at the request of one of its members or at the request of the European Commission. The President draws up a provisional agenda for each meeting, consisting of a Part A and a Part B.

The Council only discusses and reaches decisions on documents and drafts which are available in the 23 official languages (Bulgarian, Czech, Danish, Dutch, English, Estonian, Finnish, French, German, Greek, Hungarian, Irish, Italian, Latvian, Lithuanian, Maltese, Polish, Portuguese, Romanian, Slovak, Slovenian, Spanish and Swedish). If a matter is urgent, this rule may be dispensed with by unanimous agreement. This also applies to proposals for amendments tabled and discussed in the course of a meeting.

Meetings at which the Council discusses or votes on legislative proposals are open to the public. In practice, this means that the meetings are transmitted to rooms with a live audiovisual feed in the Council building.

It is in the Council that the individual interests of the Member States and the Union interest are balanced. Even though the Member States primarily defend their own interests in the Council, its members are at the same time obliged to take into account the objectives and needs of the Union as a whole. The Council is a Union institution and not an Intergovernmental Conference. Consequently it is not the lowest common denominator between the Member States that is sought in the Council's deliberations, but rather the right balance between the Union's and the Member States' interests.

Decision-making procedures

Under the EU Treaties, majority voting is applied in the Council — as a general rule, a qualified majority is sufficient (Article 16(3) TEU). A simple majority, where each Council member has one vote, is applied only in individual cases and in less sensitive areas. (A simple majority is therefore currently achieved with 14 votes).

The methods for calculating the qualified majority will change in various stages.

Up until 1 November 2014, the weighted voting system introduced by the Treaty of Nice and giving large Member States more influence will be used. Under this system, a qualified majority is achieved when there is a majority of Member States with at least 255 votes out of 345, although one Member State can also demand that these Member States represent at least 62 % of the EU population.

Since 1 January 2007 the number of votes each Member State can cast has been as follows.

WEIGHTING OF VOTES			
GERMANY	29	AUSTRIA	10
FRANCE	29	SWEDEN	10
ITALY	29	DENMARK	7
UNITED KINGDOM	29	IRELAND	7
SPAIN	27	LITHUANIA	7
POLAND	27	SLOVAKIA	7
ROMANIA	14	FINLAND	7
NETHERLANDS	13	ESTONIA	4
BELGIUM	12	CYPRUS	4
CZECH REPUBLIC	12	LATVIA	4
GREECE	12	LUXEMBOURG	4
HUNGARY	12	SLOVENIA	4
PORTUGAL	12	MALTA	3
BULGARIA	10		

On 1 November 2014 the new double majority system comes into force, under which a qualified majority is achieved when at least 55 % of the Member States representing 65 % of the EU population vote for a legislative proposal. To prevent less populous Member States from blocking the adoption of a decision, a blocking minority must consist of at least four Member States, and, if this number is not achieved, a qualified majority is deemed achieved even if the population criterion is not met. The system is complemented by a mechanism very similar to the 'Ioannina compromise': if a blocking minority is not achieved, the decision-making process can be suspended. In this case, the Council does not proceed with the vote, but continues negotiations for a reasonable period of time, if requested by Members of the Council representing at least 75 % of the population or at least 75 % of the number of Member States required for a blocking minority.

From 1 April 2017 the same mechanism will apply, but the percentages for the establishment of a blocking minority will change to at least 55 % of the population or at least 55 % of the number of Member States. The Council can amend this system *de jure* by a simple majority. However, one of the protocols stipulates that negotiations must first be held in the European Council, and that any decision made in that regard must be unanimous.

The importance of majority voting lies not so much in the fact that it prevents small States from blocking important decisions, as that it makes it possible to outvote individual large Member States. However, the 'Luxembourg Agreement' remains a major political factor, at least as far as voting practice is concerned. It grants the right to veto a Community measure in cases where a Member State considers that its vital national interests are at stake, and was used to solve a crisis which arose in 1965 when France, afraid that its national interests in the financing of the common agricultural policy were threatened, blocked decision-making in the Council for over six months by a 'policy of the empty chair'.

In the case of decisions to be taken in especially sensitive political areas, the Treaties require unanimity. The adoption of a decision cannot be blocked by means of abstentions, however. Unanimity is still required for decisions on such matters as taxes, the rights and obligations of employees, amendments to citizenship provisions and determining whether a Member State has infringed constitutional principles, and for laying down principles and guidelines in the areas of common foreign and security policy or police and judicial cooperation in criminal matters.

The High Representative of the Union for Foreign Affairs and Security Policy (Article 18 TEU)

The High Representative of the Union for Foreign Affairs and Security Policy has not become the EU foreign minister, as planned in the constitutional project; however, their position within the institutional set-up has been considerably strengthened and expanded. Initially, the office of High Representative will be merged with that of Commissioner for Foreign Affairs. This gives the High Representative a base in both the Council, where they hold the presidency of the Foreign Affairs Council, and the Commission, where they are Vice-President in charge of foreign affairs. The High Representative is appointed by the European Council, acting by a qualified majority, with the agreement of the President of the Commission. He or she is assisted by a newly created foreign service, made up of officials from the European Commission (⁵) and the General Secretariat of the Council and seconded representatives of the diplomatic services of the Member States.

(⁵) *Baroness Catherine Ashton, previously the Commissioner for Trade, was appointed to this post.*

The European Commission (Article 17 TEU)

COMPOSITION

27 Members
including President
First Vice-President: High Representative of
the Union for Foreign Affairs and Security Policy
6 Vice-Presidents

It was originally agreed that from 2014 the European Commission would no longer have a representative from each Member State, but would have a number of Members corresponding to two thirds of the number of Member States, i.e. for the current total of 27 Member States, the number of Members of the Commission in 2014 would be 18. To this end, a rotation system would be introduced to ensure that there would be a Commissioner from each Member State in two out of any three consecutive Commission periods of office. However, the European Council was given the power to change this composition by unanimous vote, and it notified its intention to do so in the conclusions of its meeting of 18 and 19 June 2009 in Brussels. At that meeting, the European Council agreed to take a decision following the entry into force of the Lisbon Treaty and in accordance with the necessary legal procedures, under which the Commission will continue to have a national from every Member State. This met one of the basic requirements set by Ireland when it organised its second referendum on the Lisbon Treaty.

Composition

The Commission is headed by a President who is assisted by seven Vice-Presidents, including the High Representative of the Union for Foreign Affairs and Security Policy as the first Vice-President. Over time, the President's position within the Commission has been considerably strengthened. He or she is no longer 'first among equals' but enjoys a prominent position in that the Commission must work 'under the political guidance' of its President (Article 17 TEU). The President thus has a 'power to provide guidance'. The President decides as to the internal organisation of the Commission in order to ensure that it acts consistently and efficiently. He or she also allocates responsibilities among the Commissioners, and may reshuffle the allocation of those responsibilities during the Commission's term of office. The President appoints the Vice-Presidents, and can force a Member of the Commission to resign. The prominent position of the President is also reflected by his or her membership of the European Council.

The President and Members of the Commission are appointed for a term of five years using the investiture procedure: the European Council, acting by a qualified majority, nominates the person it intends to propose for election by the European Parliament as President of the Commission, taking into account the majority vote of the European Parliament. The European Parliament then elects the President by a majority of its members. If the candidate does not obtain the required majority in Parliament, the European Council proposes a new candidate to Parliament within a month. The Member States then draw up a list of people to be nominated as Members of the Commission. This list is adopted by the Council, acting by a qualified majority and by common accord with the President. Once the Commission President has been elected by the European Parliament, the other Members of the Commission are subject to a vote of approval by Parliament. After approval by Parliament, the Members of the Commission other than the President are formally appointed by the Council of the EU, acting by a qualified majority.

The Members of the Commission must be chosen 'on the grounds of their general competence' and be 'completely independent in the performance of their duties' (Article 17(3) TEU). They may neither seek nor take instructions from any government.

The seat of the European Commission is in Brussels.

Tasks

Tasks	
Initiating Union legislation	Monitoring observance and proper application of Union law
Administering and implementing Union legislation	Representing the EU in international organisations

The Commission is first of all the 'driving force' behind Union policy. It is the starting point for every Union action, as it is the Commission that has to present proposals and drafts for Union legislation to the Council (this is termed the Commission's right of initiative). The Commission is not free to choose its own activities. It is obliged to act if the Union interest so requires. The Council (Article 241 TFEU), the European Parliament (Article 225 TFEU) and a group of EU citizens acting on behalf of a citizens' initiative (Article 11(4) TEU) may also ask the Commission to draw up a proposal. Since the Treaty of Lisbon, in the specific cases provided for by the Treaties, legislative acts may be adopted on the initiative of a group of Member States or of the European Parliament, on a recommendation from the European Central Bank or at the request of the Court of Justice or the European Investment Bank.

The Commission has primary powers to initiate legislation in certain areas (such as the Union budget, the Structural Funds, measures to tackle tax discrimination, the provision of funding and safeguard clauses). Much more extensive, however, are the powers for the implementation of Union rules conferred on the Commission by the Council and Parliament (Article 290 TFEU).

The Commission is also the 'guardian of Union law'. It monitors the Member States' application and implementation of primary and secondary Union legislation, institutes infringement proceedings in the event of any violation of Union law (Article 258 TFEU) and, if necessary, refers the matter to the Court of Justice. The Commission also intervenes if Union law is infringed by any natural or legal person, and imposes heavy penalties. Over the last few years, efforts to prevent abuse of Union rules have become a major part of the Commission's work.

Closely connected with the role of guardian is the task of representing the Union's interests. As a matter of principle, the Commission may serve no interests other than those of the Union. It must constantly endeavour, in what often prove to be difficult negotiations within the Council, to make the Union interest prevail and seek compromise solutions that take account of that interest. In so doing, it also plays the role of mediator between the Member States, a role for which, by virtue of its neutrality, it is particularly suited and qualified.

Lastly, the Commission is — albeit to a limited extent — an executive body. This is especially true in the field of competition law, where the Commission acts as a normal administrative authority, checking facts, granting approval or issuing bans and, if necessary, imposing penalties. The Commission's powers in relation to the Structural Funds and the EU budget are similarly wide-ranging. As a rule, however, it is the Member States themselves that have to ensure that Union rules are applied in individual cases. This solution chosen by the Union Treaties has the advantage that citizens are brought closer to what is still to them the 'foreign' reality of the European system through the workings and in the familiar form of their own national system.

The Commission represents the Union in international organisations and is in charge of the day-to-day running of Union diplomatic missions outside and within the EU. On the basis of powers conferred on it by the Council, the Commission is responsible for negotiating agreements with international organisations and non-member countries, including Accession Treaties with new Member States. The Commission represents the Union in the courts of the Member States and — where necessary together with the Council — before the Court of Justice.

ADMINISTRATIVE STRUCTURE OF THE EUROPEAN COMMISSION

Commission
(27 Members)
(Cabinets)
Secretariat General
Legal Service
Directorate-General for Communication
Bureau of European Policy Advisers

Directorate-General for Economic and Financial Affairs

Directorate-General for Enterprise and Industry

Directorate-General for Competition

Directorate-General for Employment, Social Affairs and Equal Opportunities

Directorate-General for Agriculture and Rural Development

Directorate-General for Energy

Directorate-General for Mobility and Transport

Directorate-General for the Environment

Directorate-General for Climate Action

Directorate-General for Research

Joint Research Centre

Directorate-General for the Information Society and Media
Directorate-General for Maritime Affairs and Fisheries
Directorate-General for the Internal Market and Services
Directorate-General for Regional Policy
Directorate-General for Taxation and Customs Union
Directorate-General for Education and Culture
Directorate-General for Health and Consumers
Directorate-General for Justice, Freedom and Security
Directorate-General for External Relations
Directorate-General for Trade
Directorate-General for Development
Directorate-General for Enlargement
EuropeAid Co-operation Office
Directorate-General for Humanitarian Aid (ECHO)
Eurostat
Directorate-General for Human Resources and Security
Directorate-General for Informatics
Directorate-General for the Budget
Internal Audit Office
European Anti-Fraud Office
Directorate-General for Interpretation
Directorate-General for Translation
Publications Office
Office for Infrastructure and Logistics in Brussels
Office for Infrastructure and Logistics in Luxembourg
Office for the Administration and Payment of Individual Entitlements
European Personnel Selection Office

The Court of Justice of the European Union (Article 19 TEU)

Any system will endure only if its rules are supervised by an independent authority. What is more, in a union of states the common rules — if they are subject to control by the national courts — are interpreted and applied differently from one state to another. The uniform application of Union law in all Member States would thus be jeopardised. These considerations led to the establishment of a Community Court of Justice in 1952, as soon as the

1 November 1992.
This photo of a suitcase on a map of Europe illustrates the free
movement of people, introduced by the Maastricht Treaty.

first Community (the ECSC) was created. In 1957 it also then became the judicial body for the other two Communities (E(E)C and Euratom). Today it is the judicial body of the EU.

The judicial work is now carried out on three levels by:

- the Court of Justice as the highest instance in the Community legal order (Article 253 TFEU);

- the General Court (Article 254 TFEU);

- the specialised courts, which may be appointed to the General Court to decide on cases in particular areas (Article 257 TFEU).

Court of Justice

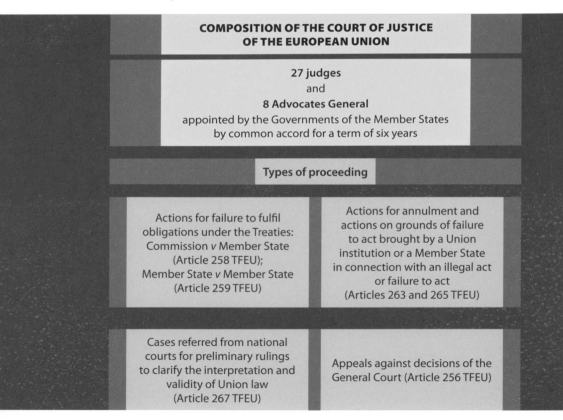

**COMPOSITION OF THE COURT OF JUSTICE
OF THE EUROPEAN UNION**

27 judges
and
8 Advocates General
appointed by the Governments of the Member States
by common accord for a term of six years

Types of proceeding

Actions for failure to fulfil obligations under the Treaties: Commission *v* Member State (Article 258 TFEU); Member State *v* Member State (Article 259 TFEU)

Actions for annulment and actions on grounds of failure to act brought by a Union institution or a Member State in connection with an illegal act or failure to act (Articles 263 and 265 TFEU)

Cases referred from national courts for preliminary rulings to clarify the interpretation and validity of Union law (Article 267 TFEU)

Appeals against decisions of the General Court (Article 256 TFEU)

The Court of Justice currently consists of 27 judges and eight Advocates General, who are appointed 'by common accord of the Governments of the Member States' for a term of six years. Each Member State sends one judge. In order to ensure a degree of continuity, partial replacement of half the judges and Advocates General takes place every three years at the beginning of the judicial year on 6 October. They may be reappointed.

The Court is assisted by eight Advocates General, whose term of office corresponds to that of the judges; they enjoy judicial independence. Four of the eight Advocates General are always from the 'large' Member States (Germany, France, Italy and the United Kingdom) and the other four come from the remaining 23 Member States on an alternating basis. The office of Advocate General is based on that of the *Commissaire du gouvernement* in the Council of State (*Conseil d'État*) and administrative courts in France. It must not be confused with the position of public prosecutor or similar post found in many countries. Advocates General were introduced in the Court to counterbalance the original 'single-tier' nature of court proceedings, i.e. the absence of any appeal procedures. Their task is to submit 'opinions' to the Court in the form of (non-binding) proposals for a Court decision based on a fully independent and non-partisan survey of the questions of law raised in the case concerned. The opinions are an integral part of the oral procedure and are published together with the judgment in the Court Reports. Advocates General can only influence the judgment through the strength of the arguments in their opinions; they are not involved in any deliberations or voting on the judgment.

Selection of judges and Advocates General

The judges and Advocates General are chosen from persons whose independence is beyond doubt and who possess the qualifications required for appointment to the highest judicial offices in their respective countries, or who are legal experts of recognised competence (Article 253 TFEU). This means that judges, public officials, politicians, lawyers or university lecturers from Member States may be appointed. The variety of professional backgrounds and experience are beneficial to the Court in that they help to provide as comprehensive an assessment as possible of both the theoretical and practical aspects of the facts and points of law that have to be considered. In all Member States, the choice of who should be proposed by the government for appointment as a judge or Advocate General, and the procedure by which this is done, is a matter for the executive. The procedures differ greatly and range from the not very transparent to the totally impenetrable.

Assistance is provided by the newly created consultative panel for the nomination of judges, which has the task of giving an opinion on candidates' suitability to perform the duties of judge and Advocate General of the Court of Justice and the General Court before the governments of the Member States make the appointments (Article 255 TFEU). The panel comprises seven persons chosen from among former members of the Court of Justice and the General Court, members of national supreme courts and lawyers of recognised competence, one of whom is proposed by the European Parliament.

Procedure

The Court sits in the following possible formations:

- the full Court with 27 judges; a full Court decision is still required only in impeachment proceedings and disciplinary proceedings against members of the Union bodies. Cases may also be referred to the full Court by the Court of Justice itself, but only where extremely important proceedings and matters of precedent are involved;

- the Grand Chamber with 13 judges;

- Chambers of five and three judges.

Tasks

The Court of Justice is the highest and at the same time the sole judicial authority in matters of Union law. In general terms, its task is to 'ensure that in the interpretation of [the] Treaty the law is observed'.

This general description of responsibilities encompasses three main areas:

- monitoring the application of Union law, both by the EU institutions when implementing the Treaties, and by the Member States and individuals in relation to their obligations under Union law;

- interpretation of Union law;

- further shaping of Union law.

In carrying out these tasks, the Court's work involves both legal advice and adjudication. Legal advice is provided in the form of binding opinions on agreements which the EU wishes to conclude with non-member countries or international organisations. Its function as a body for the administration of justice is much more important, however. In exercising that function, it operates in matters that in the Member States would be assigned to different types of court, depending on their national systems. It acts as a constitutional court when disputes between Union institutions are before it or legislative instruments are up for review for legality; as an administrative court when reviewing the administrative acts of the Commission or of national authorities applying Union legislation; as a labour court or industrial tribunal when dealing with freedom of movement, social security and equal opportunities; as a fiscal court when dealing with matters concerning the validity and interpretation of directives in the fields of taxation and customs law; as a criminal court when reviewing Commission decisions imposing fines; and as a civil court when hearing claims for damages or interpreting the provisions on the enforcement of judgments in civil and commercial matters and in disputes over European intellectual property rights for which grounds for jurisdiction by the Court of Justice have been given (Article 262 TFEU).

The General Court

Like all courts, the Court of Justice is overburdened. The number of cases referred to it has increased steadily and will continue to grow, given the potential for disputes that has been created by the huge number of directives which have been adopted in the context of the single market and transposed into national law in the Member States. The signs are already there that the Treaty on European Union has raised further questions which will ultimately have to be settled by the Court. This is why, in 1988, a General Court was established to take the pressure off the Court of Justice.

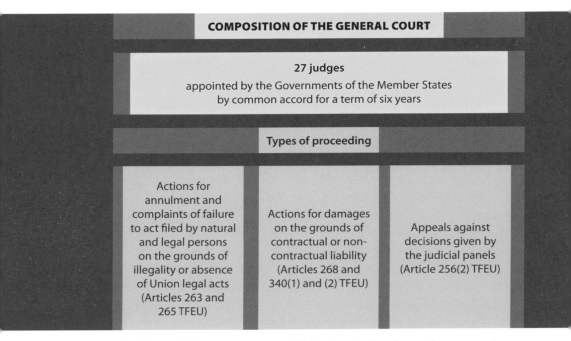

COMPOSITION OF THE GENERAL COURT

27 judges
appointed by the Governments of the Member States
by common accord for a term of six years

Types of proceeding

Actions for annulment and complaints of failure to act filed by natural and legal persons on the grounds of illegality or absence of Union legal acts (Articles 263 and 265 TFEU)	Actions for damages on the grounds of contractual or non-contractual liability (Articles 268 and 340(1) and (2) TFEU)	Appeals against decisions given by the judicial panels (Article 256(2) TFEU)

The General Court is not a new Union institution but rather a constituent component of the Court of Justice. Nevertheless, it is an autonomous body separate from the Court of Justice in organisational terms. It has its own registry and rules of procedure. Cases handled by the General Court are identified by means of a 'T' (= Tribunal) (e.g. T-1/99), whilst those referred to the Court of Justice are coded with a 'C' (= Court) (e.g. C-1/99).

The General Court consists of 27 'members' whose qualifications, appointment and legal status are subject to the same requirements and conditions as judges at the Court of Justice. Although their main function is to sit as 'judges', they may also be appointed as 'Advocates General' on an ad hoc basis in cases before the full Court, or in cases before one of the Chambers if the facts of the case or its legal complexity require this. This facility has been used very sparingly up to now.

The General Court sits in Chambers of five or three judges or, in certain cases, a single judge. It can also sit as a Grand Chamber (13 judges) or as a full Court (27 judges) if required by the legal complexity or significance of a case. Over 80 % of the cases before the Court are heard by a Chamber of three judges.

Although the General Court was originally responsible for only a limited range of cases, it now has the following tasks.

- At first instance, i.e. subject to the legal supervision of the Court of Justice, the General Court has competence to rule on actions for annulment and actions for failure to act brought by natural and legal persons against a Union body, on an arbitration clause contained in a contract concluded by the EU or on its behalf, and on actions for damages brought against the EU.

- The General Court acts as an appeal court for cases of appeal against decisions given by the judicial panels.

- It is also planned to confer jurisdiction on the General Court for preliminary ruling proceedings concerning certain areas; however, this option has not yet been used.

Specialised courts

In 2004, to relieve the burden on the Court of Justice and improve legal protection in the EU, the Council of the EU attached a specialised court for civil service cases to the General Court.

This specialised court has taken over jurisdiction from the General Court for ruling at first instance in European civil service disputes.

It consists of seven judges, who enjoy a similar status to members of the General Court and are appointed for a term of six years. They must have the ability required for appointment to judicial office. The specialised court usually sits as a panel of three judges, but can give a decision as a full panel or a panel of five judges, or as a single judge. Decisions of the specialised court are subject to a right of appeal to the General Court on points of law only. In turn, the First Advocate General (not the parties involved!) can propose a review of the decision of the General Court if the legal entity or the uniformity of jurisprudence are jeopardised.

The European Central Bank (Articles 129 and 130 TFEU)

The European Central Bank (ECB), based in Frankfurt-am-Main, is at the heart of economic and monetary union. Its task is to maintain the stability of the European currency, the euro, and control the amount of currency in circulation (Article 128 TFEU).

In order to carry out this task, the ECB's independence is guaranteed by numerous legal provisions. When exercising their powers or carrying out their tasks and duties, neither the ECB nor a national central bank may take instructions from Union institutions, governments of Member States or any other body. The EU institutions and the Member States' governments will not seek to influence the ECB (Article 130 TFEU).

The ECB has a Governing Council and an Executive Board. The Governing Council comprises the governors of the central banks of the 16 Member States in the euro area and the members of the Executive Board of the ECB. The Executive Board, which is made up of the President, the Vice-President and four other members, is effectively in charge of running the ECB. Its President and members are appointed from among persons of recognised standing and experience in monetary or banking matters by common accord of the governments of the Member States, on a recommendation from the Council after it has consulted the European Parliament. Their term of office is eight years, which, in the interests of ensuring the independence of the Executive Board members, is not renewable (Article 283 TFEU).

The European System of Central Banks (ESCB) is composed of the ECB and the central banks of the Member States (Article 129 TFEU). It has the task of defining and implementing the monetary policy of the Union, and has the exclusive right to authorise the issue of banknotes and coins within the Union. It also manages the official currency reserves of the Member States and ensures the smooth operation of payments systems (Article 127(2) TFEU).

The Court of Auditors (Articles 285 and 286 TFEU)

The Court of Auditors was set up on 22 July 1975 and began work in Luxembourg in October 1977. It has since risen to the rank of Union institution (Article 13 TEU). It consists of 27 members, corresponding to the present number of Member States. They are appointed for six years by the Council, which approves, by qualified majority and following consultation with the European Parliament, a list of members drawn up in accordance with proposals from the Member States (Article 286(2) TFEU). The members elect the President of the Court of Auditors from among their number for a term of three years; the President may be re-elected.

The Court of Auditors' task is to examine whether all revenue has been received and all expenditure incurred in a lawful and regular manner and whether financial management has been sound. Unlike the courts of auditors or similar bodies in some Member States, it has no jurisdiction to enforce its control measures or to investigate suspicions of irregularity arising from its investigations. However, it is wholly autonomous in its decisions regarding what it examines and how. It can, for instance, examine whether the use made of Union financial support by private individuals is in compliance with Community law.

The chief weapon in its armoury is the fact that it can publicise its findings. The results of its investigations are summarised in an annual report at the end of each financial year, which is published in the *Official Journal of the European Union* and thus brought to public attention. It may also make special reports at any time on specific areas of financial management, and these are also published in the Official Journal.

ADVISORY BODIES

European Economic and Social Committee (Article 301 TFEU)

The purpose of the European Economic and Social Committee (EESC) is to give the various economic and social groups (especially employers and employees, farmers, carriers, business people, craft workers, the professions and managers of small and medium-sized businesses) representation in an EU institution. It also provides a forum for consumers, environmental groups and associations.

The EESC is made up of a maximum of 350 members (advisers), drawn from the most representative organisations in the individual Member States. They are appointed for five years by the Council, which, acting in unanimity, adopts a list of members drawn up in accordance with the proposals made by each Member State.

The allocation of seats is as follows ([6]).

GERMANY	24
FRANCE	24
ITALY	24
UNITED KINGDOM	24
SPAIN	21
POLAND	21
ROMANIA	15
BELGIUM	12
BULGARIA	12
CZECH REPUBLIC	12
GREECE	12
HUNGARY	12
NETHERLANDS	12
AUSTRIA	12
PORTUGAL	12
SWEDEN	12
DENMARK	9
IRELAND	9
LITHUANIA	9
SLOVAKIA	9
FINLAND	9
ESTONIA	7
LATVIA	7
SLOVENIA	7
CYPRUS	6
LUXEMBOURG	6
MALTA	5

The members are divided up into three groups (employers, workers and other parties representative of civil society). Opinions to be adopted at plenary sessions are drawn up by 'study groups' consisting of EESC members (in which

---

([6]) *Source: Website of the European Economic and Social Committee; 344 members in March 2010.*

their alternates may also participate as experts). The EESC also works closely with the committees of the European Parliament.

The EESC, which was established under the Treaties of Rome, must in certain circumstances be consulted by the Council acting on a proposal from the Commission. It also issues opinions on its own initiative. These opinions represent a synthesis of sometimes very divergent viewpoints and are extremely useful for the Commission and the Council because they show what changes the groups directly affected by a proposal would like to see. The EESC's own-initiative opinions have on a number of occasions had considerable political implications, one example being that of 22 February 1989 on basic social rights in the EU, which provided the basis for the 'Social Charter' proposed by the Commission (and adopted by 11 Member States).

Committee of the Regions (Article 305 TFEU)

A new advisory body was set up alongside the EESC by the Treaty on European Union (Treaty of Maastricht): the Committee of the Regions (CoR). Like the EESC, it is not strictly an EU institution, as its function is purely advisory and it has no power to produce legally binding decisions in the same way as the fully fledged institutions (European Parliament, Council, European Commission, Court of Justice, Court of Auditors, European Central Bank).

Like the EESC, the Committee of the Regions consists of a maximum of 350 members ([7]). The members are representatives of regional and local authorities in the Member States who must have a mandate based on elections from the authorities they represent, or must be politically accountable to them. The 350 seats are allocated to the Member States using the same weighting as for the EESC. The members are appointed for five years by the Council, which, acting in unanimity, adopts a list of members drawn up in accordance with the proposals made by each Member State. The members of the Committee elect a chairman from among their number for a term of two years.

There are a number of areas in which consultation by the Council of the EU or the European Commission is required ('mandatory consultation'):

([7]) *Source: Website of the Committee of the Regions; 344 members in March 2010.*

education; culture; public health; trans-European networks; transport, tele-communications and energy infrastructure; economic and social cohesion; employment policy and social legislation. The Council also consults the Committee regularly, and without any legal obligation, in connection with a wide range of draft legislation ('non-mandatory consultation').

THE EUROPEAN INVESTMENT BANK (ARTICLE 308 TFEU)

As financing agency for a 'balanced and steady development' of the EU, the Union has at its disposal the European Investment Bank (EIB), located in Luxembourg. The EIB provides loans and guarantees in all economic sectors, especially to promote the development of less-developed regions, to modernise or convert undertakings or create new jobs and to assist projects of common interest to several Member States.

The EIB has a tripartite structure: it is headed by the Board of Governors, made up of the Finance Ministers of the Member States, which sets the guidelines for credit policy and authorises EIB activities outside the EU. The Board of Governors is followed by the Board of Directors, which has 28 full members (one representative from each of the Member States and one from the European Commission) and 18 alternate members. Members are usually senior officials from the national finance or economic affairs ministries. The Board of Directors takes decisions in respect of granting loans and guarantees and raising loans. It makes sure that the bank is run in accordance with the guidelines of the Board of Governors. The day-to-day activities of the EIB are run by the Management Committee, an executive of nine persons appointed for a period of six years.

The legal order of the EU

The constitution of the EU described above, and particularly the fundamental values it embodies, can be brought to life and given substance only through Union law. This makes the EU a legal reality in two different senses: it is created by law and is a community based on law.

THE EU AS A CREATION OF LAW AND A COMMUNITY BASED ON LAW

This is what is entirely new about the EU, and what distinguishes it from earlier attempts to unite Europe. It works not by means of force or subjugation but simply by means of law. Law is intended to achieve what 'blood and iron' have for centuries failed to bring about. For only unity based on a freely made decision can be expected to last: unity founded on the fundamental values such as freedom and equality, and protected and translated into reality by law. That is the insight underlying the Treaties that created the European Union.

However, the EU is not merely a creation of law but also pursues its objectives purely by means of law. It is a community based on law. The common economic and social life of the peoples of the Member States is governed not by the threat of force but by the law of the Union. This is the basis of the institutional system. It lays down the procedure for decision-making by the Union institutions and regulates their relationship to each other. It provides the institutions with the means — in the shape of regulations, directives and decisions — of enacting legal instruments binding on the Member States and their citizens. Thus the individuals themselves become a main focus of the Union. Its legal order directly affects their daily life to an ever-increasing extent. It accords them rights and imposes obligations on them, so that as citizens both of their State and of the Union they are governed by a hierarchy of legal orders — a phenomenon familiar from federal constitutions. Like any legal order, that of the EU provides a self-contained system of legal protection for the purpose of recourse to and the enforcement of Union law. Union law also defines the relationship between the EU and the Member States.

The Member States must take all appropriate measures to ensure fulfilment of the obligations arising from the Treaties or resulting from action taken by the institutions of the Union. They must facilitate the achievement of the EU's tasks and abstain from any measure that could jeopardise the attainment of the objectives of the Treaties. The Member States are answerable to the citizens of the EU for any harm caused through violations of Union law.

THE LEGAL SOURCES OF UNION LAW

The term 'legal source' has two meanings: in its original meaning, it refers to the reason for the emergence of a legal provision, i.e. the motivation behind the creation of a legal construct. According to this definition, the 'legal source' of Union law is the will to preserve peace and create a better Europe through closer economic ties, two cornerstones of the EC. In legal parlance, on the other hand, 'legal source' refers to the origin and embodiment of the law.

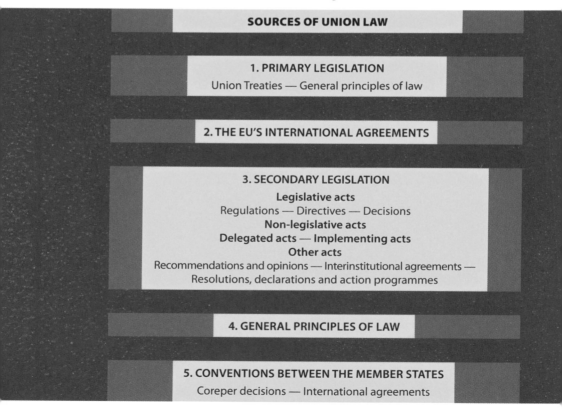

SOURCES OF UNION LAW

1. PRIMARY LEGISLATION
Union Treaties — General principles of law

2. THE EU'S INTERNATIONAL AGREEMENTS

3. SECONDARY LEGISLATION
Legislative acts
Regulations — Directives — Decisions
Non-legislative acts
Delegated acts — Implementing acts
Other acts
Recommendations and opinions — Interinstitutional agreements —
Resolutions, declarations and action programmes

4. GENERAL PRINCIPLES OF LAW

5. CONVENTIONS BETWEEN THE MEMBER STATES
Coreper decisions — International agreements

THE EU FOUNDING TREATIES AS THE PRIMARY SOURCE OF UNION LAW

The first source of Union law in this sense is the EU founding Treaties, with the various annexes, appendices and protocols attached to them, and later additions and amendments. These founding Treaties and the instruments amending and supplementing them (chiefly the Treaties of Maastricht, Amsterdam, Nice and Lisbon) and the various Accession Treaties contain the basic provisions on the EU's objectives, organisation and modus operandi, and parts of its economic law. They thus set the constitutional framework for the life of the EU, which is then fleshed out in the Union's interest by legislative and administrative action by the Union institutions. The Treaties, being legal instruments created directly by the Member States, are known in legal circles as primary Union law.

THE EU LEGAL INSTRUMENTS AS THE SECONDARY SOURCE OF UNION LAW

Law made by the Union institutions through exercising the powers conferred on them is referred to as secondary legislation, the second important source of EU law.

It consists of legislative acts, delegated acts, implementing acts and other legal acts. 'Legislative acts' are legal acts adopted by ordinary or special legislative procedure (Article 289 TFEU). 'Delegated acts' are non-legislative acts of general and binding application to supplement or amend certain non-essential elements of a legislative act. They are adopted by the Commission; a legislative act must be drawn up explicitly delegating power to the Commission for this purpose. The objectives, content, scope and duration of the delegation of power are explicitly defined in the legislative act concerned. This delegation of power can be revoked by the Council or the European Parliament at any time. A delegated act may enter into force only if no objection has been raised by the European Parliament or the Council within a period set by the legislative act (Article 290 TFEU). 'Implementing acts' are an exception to the principle whereby all the measures required to implement binding EU legal acts are taken by the Member States in accordance with their own national provisions. Where uniform conditions are needed for implementing legally binding EU acts, this is done by means of appropriate implementing acts, which are generally adopted by the Commission, and, in certain exceptional cases, by the Council. However, the European Parliament and the Council lay down in advance the rules and general principles concerning the mechanisms for control by Member States of the Commission's exercise of implementing powers (Article 291 TFEU). Finally, there is a whole set of 'other legal acts' which the Union institutions can use to issue non-binding measures and statements or which regulate the internal workings of the EU or its institutions, such as agreements or arrangements between the institutions, or internal rules of procedure.

These legal acts can take very different forms. The most important of these are listed and defined in Article 288 TFEU. As binding legal acts, they include both general and abstract legal provisions on the one hand and specific, individual measures on the other. They also provide for the Union institutions to issue non-binding statements. This list of acts is not exhaustive, however. Many other legal acts do not fit into specific categories. These include resolutions, declarations, action programmes or White and Green Papers. There are considerable differences between the various acts in terms of the procedure involved, their legal effect and those to whom they are addressed; these differences will be dealt with in more detail in the section on the 'means of action'.

The creation of secondary Union legislation is a gradual process. Its emergence lends vitality to the primary legislation deriving from the Union Treaties, and progressively generates and enhances the European legal order.

INTERNATIONAL AGREEMENTS OF THE EU

A third source of Union law is connected with the EU's role at the international level. As one of the focal points of the world, Europe cannot confine itself to managing its own internal affairs; it has to concern itself with economic, social and political relations with the world outside. The EU therefore concludes agreements in international law with non-member countries ('third countries') and with other international organisations; these range from treaties providing for extensive cooperation in trade or in the industrial, technical and social fields, to agreements on trade in particular products.

Three kinds of agreement between the EU and non-member countries are particularly worth mentioning.

Association agreements

Association goes far beyond the mere regulation of trade policy and involves close economic cooperation and wide-ranging financial assistance from the EU for the country concerned (Article 217 TFEU). A distinction may be drawn between three different types of association agreement.

Agreements that maintain special links between certain Member States and non-member countries

One particular reason for the creation of the association agreement was the existence of countries and territories outside Europe with which Belgium, Denmark, France, Italy, the Netherlands and the United Kingdom maintained particularly close economic ties as a legacy of their colonial past. The introduction of a common external tariff in the EU would have seriously disrupted trade with these territories, which meant that special arrangements were needed. The purpose of association is therefore to promote the economic and social development of the countries and territories and to establish close economic relations between them and the Union as a whole (Article 198 TFEU). As a result, there are a whole range of preferential agreements enabling goods to be imported from these countries and territories at reduced or zero customs rates. Financial and technical assistance from the EU was channelled through the European Development Fund. Far and away the most important agreement in practice is the EU–ACP Partnership Agreement between the EU and 70 States in Africa, the Caribbean and the Pacific ('the ACP'). This agreement was recently converted into a set of economic partnership agreements, gradually giving the ACP countries free access to the European internal market.

Agreements as preparation for accession to the Union or for the establishment of a customs union

Association arrangements are also used in the preparation of countries for possible membership of the Union. The arrangement serves as a preliminary stage towards accession during which the applicant country can work on converging its economy with that of the EU.

Agreement on the European Economic Area (EEA)

The EEA Agreement brings the (remaining) countries in the European Free Trade Association (EFTA) (Iceland, Liechtenstein and Norway) into the internal market and, by requiring them to incorporate nearly two thirds of the EU's legislation, lays a firm basis for subsequent accession. In the EEA, on the basis of the *acquis communautaire* (the body of primary and secondary Union

legislation), there is to be free movement of goods, persons, services and capital, uniform rules on competition and state aid, and closer cooperation on horizontal and flanking policies (environment, research and development, education).

Cooperation agreements

Cooperation agreements are not as far-reaching as association agreements, being aimed solely at intensive economic cooperation. The EU has such agreements with the Maghreb States (Algeria, Morocco and Tunisia), the Mashreq States (Egypt, Jordan, Lebanon and Syria) and Israel, for instance.

Trade agreements

The Union also has a considerable number of trade agreements with individual non-member countries, with groupings of such countries or within international trade organisations relating to tariffs and trade policy. The most important international trade agreements are: the Agreement establishing the World Trade Organisation (WTO Agreement) and the multilateral trade agreements deriving from it, including in particular the General Agreement on Tariffs and Trade (GATT 1994); the Antidumping and Subsidies Code, the General Agreement on Trade in Services (GATS); the Agreement on Trade-Related Aspects of Intellectual Property Rights (TRIPS); and the Understanding on Rules and Procedures Governing the Settlement of Disputes.

SOURCES OF UNWRITTEN LAW

The sources of Union law described so far share a common feature in that they all produce written law. Like all systems of law, however, the EU legal order cannot consist entirely of written rules: there will always be gaps which have to be filled by unwritten law.

General principles of law

The unwritten sources of Union law are the general principles of law. These are rules reflecting the elementary concepts of law and justice that must be respected by any legal system. Written Union law for the most part deals only with economic and social matters, and is only to a limited extent capable of laying down rules of this kind, which means that the general principles of law form one of the most important sources of law in the Union. They allow gaps to be filled and questions of the interpretation of existing law to be settled in the fairest way.

These principles are given effect when the law is applied, particularly in the judgments of the Court of Justice, which is responsible for ensuring that 'in the interpretation and application of this Treaty the law is observed'. The main points of reference for determining the general principles of law are the principles common to the legal orders of the Member States. They provide the background against which the EU rules needed for solving a problem can be developed.

Alongside the principles of autonomy, direct applicability and the primacy of Union law, other legal principles include the guarantee of basic rights, the principle of proportionality, the protection of legitimate expectations, the right to a proper hearing and the principle that the Member States are liable for infringements of Union law.

Legal custom

Unwritten Union law also encompasses legal custom. This is understood to mean a practice which has been followed and accepted and thus become legally established, and which adds to or modifies primary or secondary legislation. The possible establishment of legal custom in Union law is acknowledged in principle. There are considerable limitations on its becoming established in the context of Union law, however. The first hurdle is the existence of a special procedure for the amendment of the Treaties (Article 54 TEU). This does not rule out the possible emergence of legal custom, but it does make the criteria according to which a practice is deemed to have been followed and accepted for a substantial period much harder to meet. Another hurdle to the establishment of legal custom in the Union institutions is the fact that any action by an institution may derive its validity only from the Treaties, and not from that institution's actual conduct or any intention on its part to create legal relations. This means that, at the level of the Treaties, legal custom can under no circumstances be established by the Union institutions; at most, only the Member States can do this — and then only subject to the stringent conditions mentioned above. Procedures and practices followed and accepted as part of the law by Union institutions may, however, be drawn on when interpreting the legal rules laid down by them, which might alter the legal implications and scope of the legal act concerned. However, the conditions and limitations arising from primary Union legislation must also be borne in mind here.

Agreements between the Member States

The final source of EU law comprises agreements between the Member States. Agreements of this kind may be concluded for the settlement of issues closely linked to the EU's activities, but no powers have been transferred to the Union institutions; there are also full-scale international agreements (treaties and conventions) between the Member States aimed especially at overcoming the drawbacks of territorially limited arrangements and creating law that applies uniformly throughout the EU. This is important primarily in the field of private international law. These agreements include: the Convention on Jurisdiction and the Enforcement of Judgments in Civil and Commercial Matters (1968), which has, however, been replaced by a Council regulation of 2001, except in the case of Denmark, and is therefore now part of secondary Union legislation; the Convention on the Mutual Recognition of Companies and Legal Persons (1968); the Convention on the Elimination of Double Taxation in connection with the Adjustment of Transfers of Profits between Associated Enterprises (1990) and the Convention on the Law Applicable to Contractual Obligations (1980).

THE **EU**'S MEANS OF ACTION

The system of legislative acts had to be devised afresh when the EU was set up. It had to be decided first and foremost what forms Union legislation should take and what effects these should have. The institutions had to be able to align the disparate economic, social and not least environmental conditions in the various Member States, and do so effectively, i.e. without depending on the goodwill of the Member States, so that the best possible living conditions could be created for all the citizens of the Union. On the other hand, they were not to interfere in the domestic systems of law any more than necessary. The entire EU legislative system is therefore based on the principle that where the same arrangement, even on points of detail, must apply in all Member States, national arrangements must be replaced by Union legislation, but where this is not necessary due account must be taken of the existing legal orders in the Member States.

Against this background a range of instruments was developed that allowed the Union institutions to impact on the national legal systems to varying degrees. The most drastic action is the replacement of national rules by Union ones. There are also Union rules by which the Union institutions act on the Member States' legal systems only indirectly. Measures may also be taken that affect only a defined or identifiable addressee, in order to deal with a particular case. Lastly, provision is also made for legal acts that have no binding force, either on the Member States or on the citizens of the Union.

If we look at the range of EU legal instruments in terms of the persons to whom they are addressed and their practical effects in the Member States, they can be broken down as follows.

	ADDRESSEES	EFFECTS
REGULATION	All Member States, natural and legal persons	Directly applicable and binding in their entirety
DIRECTIVE	All or specific Member States	Binding with respect to the intended result. Directly applicable only under particular circumstances
DECISION	Not specified All or specific Member States; specific natural or legal persons	Directly applicable and binding in their entirety
RECOMMENDATION	All or specific Member States, other EU bodies, individuals	Not binding
AVIS	All or specific Member States, other EU bodies	Not binding
	Not specified	Not binding

REGULATIONS AS UNION 'LAWS'

The legal acts that enable the Union institutions to impinge furthest on the domestic legal systems are the regulations. Two features highly unusual in international law mark them out.

■ The first is their Community nature, which means that they lay down the same law throughout the Union, regardless of international borders, and apply in full in all Member States. A Member State has no power to apply a regulation incompletely or to select only those provisions of which it approves as a means of ensuring that an instrument which it opposed at the time of its adoption or which runs counter to its perceived national interest is not given effect. Nor can it invoke provisions or practices of domestic law to preclude the mandatory application of a regulation.

■ The second is direct applicability, which means that the legal acts do not have to be transposed into national law but confer rights or impose obligations on the Union citizen in the same way as national law. The Member States and their governing institutions and courts are bound directly by Union law and have to comply with it in the same way as with national law.

The similarities between these legal acts and statute law passed in individual Member States are unmistakable. If they are enacted with the involvement of the European Parliament (under the co-decision-making procedure — see next section), they are described as 'legislative acts'. Parliament has no responsibility for regulations, which are only enacted by the Council or the European Commission and thus, from a procedural point of view at least, they lack the essential characteristics of legislation of this kind.

DIRECTIVES

The directive is the most important legislative instrument alongside the regulation. Its purpose is to reconcile the dual objectives of both securing the necessary uniformity of Union law and respecting the diversity of national traditions and structures. What the directive primarily aims for, then, is not the unification of the law, which is the regulation's purpose, but its harmonisation. The idea is to remove contradictions and conflicts between national laws and regulations or gradually iron out inconsistencies so that, as far as possible, the same material conditions exist in all the Member States. The directive is one of the primary means deployed in building the single market.

A directive is binding on the Member States as regards the objective to be achieved but leaves it to the national authorities to decide on how the agreed Community objective is to be incorporated into their domestic legal systems. The reasoning behind this form of legislation is that it allows intervention in domestic economic and legal structures to take a milder form. In particular, Member States can take account of special domestic circumstances when implementing Community rules. What happens is that the directive does not supersede the laws of the Member States but places the Member States under an obligation to adapt their national law in line with Community provisions. The result is generally a two-stage law-making process.

First, at the initial stage, the directive lays down the objective that is to be achieved at EU level by any or all Member State(s) to which it is addressed within a specified time-frame. The Union institutions can actually spell out the objective in such detailed terms as to leave the Member States with no room for manoeuvre, and this has in fact been done in directives on technical standards and environmental protection.

Second, at the national stage, the objective set at EU level is translated into actual legal or administrative provisions in the Member States. Even if the Member States are in principle free to determine the form and methods used to transpose their EU obligation into domestic law, EU criteria are used to assess whether they have done so in accordance with EU law. The general principle is that a legal situation must be generated in which the rights and obligations arising from the directive can be recognised with sufficient clarity and certainty to enable the Union citizen to invoke or, if appropriate, challenge them in the national courts. This normally involves enacting mandatory provisions of national law or repealing or amending existing rules. Administrative custom on its own is not enough since it can, by its very nature, be changed at will by the authorities concerned; nor does it have a sufficiently high profile.

Directives do not as a rule directly confer rights or impose obligations on the Union citizen. They are expressly addressed to the Member States alone. Rights and obligations for the citizen flow only from the measures enacted by the authorities of the Member States to implement the directive. This point is of no importance to citizens as long as the Member States actually comply with their Union obligation. But there are disadvantages for Union citizens where a Member State does not take the requisite implementing measures to achieve an objective set in a directive that would benefit them, or where the measures taken are inadequate. The Court of Justice has refused to tolerate such disadvantages, and a long line of cases has determined that in such circumstances Union citizens can plead that the directive or recommendation has direct effect in actions in the national courts to secure the rights conferred on them by it. Direct effect is defined by the Court as follows.

- The provisions of the directive must lay down the rights of the EU citizen/undertaking with sufficient clarity and precision.

- The exercise of the rights is not conditional.

- The national legislative authorities may not be given any room for manoeuvre regarding the content of the rules to be enacted.

- The time allowed for implementation of the directive has expired.

The decisions of the Court of Justice concerning direct effect are based on the general view that the Member State is acting equivocally and unlawfully if it applies its old law without adapting it to the requirements of the directive. This is an abuse of rights by the Member State and the recognition of direct effect of the directive seeks to combat it by ensuring that the Member State derives no benefit from its violation of Union law. Direct effect thus has the effect of penalising the offending Member State. In that context it is significant that the Court of Justice has applied the principle solely in cases between citizen and Member State, and then only when the directive was for the citizen's benefit and not to their detriment — in other words when the citizen's position under the law as amended under the directive was more favourable than under the old law (known as 'vertical direct effect'). However, application of the vertical direct effect of directives does not prevent the fact that the direct effect of a directive to the benefit of an individual may be to the detriment of another individual (the dual-effect directive, which is often found in procurement and environment law). This detriment should be considered as a negative legal reflex that stems inevitably from the Member States' obligation to reconcile their legal order with the objectives of a directive at the end of the transposition period; there is no further detriment caused by recognition of the vertical effect of the directives.

The direct effect of directives in relations between citizens themselves ('horizontal direct effect') has not been accepted by the Court of Justice. The Court concludes from the punitive nature of the principle that it is not applicable to relations between private individuals, since they cannot be held liable for the consequences of the Member State's failure to act. What the citizen needs to rely on is certainty in the law and the protection of legitimate expectations. The citizen must be able to count on the effect of a directive being achieved by national implementing measures. However, in its more recent case-law, the Court of Justice has tempered its rejection of the direct effect of directive law in private-law issues. It is limited to situations in which one contracting party invokes a right stemming from the directive against a right of the other party stemming from national law. This opens the way to a horizontal application of the directly applicable provisions of directives in situations concerning, for example, compliance with objective national law (when, for example, an enterprise wishes to oblige a competitor to comply with a national law which infringes on the law of the directive) or the implementation of obligations from national law which contradict application of the directive (such as the refusal to fulfil a contract with invocation of national prohibitory provisions that infringe the law of the directive).

The direct effect of a directive does not necessarily imply that a provision of the directive confers rights on the individual. In fact, the provisions of a directive have a direct effect insofar as they have the effect of objective law. The same conditions apply to the recognition of this effect as for the recognition of a direct effect, the only exception being that, instead of clear and precise law being set out for the Union citizen or enterprise, a clear and precise obligation is established for the Member States. Where this is the case, all institutions, i.e. the legislator, administration and courts of the Member States, are bound by the directive and must automatically comply with it and apply it as Union law with primacy. In concrete terms, they also therefore have an obligation to interpret national law in accordance with the directives or give the provision of the directive in question priority of application over conflicting national law. In addition, the directives have certain limiting effects on the Member States — even before the end of the transposition period. In view of the binding nature of a directive and their duty to facilitate the achievement of the Union's tasks (Article 4 TEU), Member States must abstain, before the end of the transposition period, from any measure which could jeopardise the attainment of the objective of the directive.

In its judgments in *Francovich* and *Bonifaci* in 1991, the Court of Justice held that Member States are liable to pay damages where loss is sustained by reason of failure to transpose a directive in whole or in part. Both cases were brought against Italy for failure to transpose on time Council Directive 80/987/EEC of 20 October 1980 on the protection of employees in the event of the employer's insolvency, which sought to protect the employee's rights to remuneration in the period preceding insolvency and dismissal on grounds of insolvency. To that end, guarantee funds were to be established with protection from creditors; they were to be funded by employers, the public authorities or both. The problem facing the Court was that, although the aim of the directive was to confer on employed workers a personal right to continued payment of remuneration from the guarantee funds, this right could not be given direct effect by the national courts, meaning that they could not enforce it against the national authorities, since in the absence of measures transposing the directive the guarantee fund had not been established and it was not possible to ascertain who was the debtor in connection with the insolvency. The Court ruled that, by failing to implement the directive, Italy had deprived the employed workers in question of their rights and was accordingly liable for damages. Even if the duty to compensate is not written into Union law, the Court of Justice sees it as an integral part of the EU legal order, since its full effect would not be secured and the rights conferred by it would not be protected if Union citizens did not have the possibility of seeking and obtaining compensation for infringement of their rights by Member States acting in contravention of EU law.

DECISIONS

The third category of EU legal acts is that of decisions. In some cases the Union institutions may themselves be responsible for implementing the Treaties and regulations, and this will be possible only if they are in a position to take measures binding on particular individuals, undertakings or Member States. The situation in the Member States' own systems is more or less the same; legislation will be applied by the authorities in an individual case by means of an administrative decision.

In the EU legal order this function is assumed by decisions, which are the means normally available to the Union institutions to order that a measure be taken in an individual case. The Union institutions can thus require a Member State or an individual to perform or refrain from an action, or can confer rights or impose obligations on them.

The basic characteristics of a decision can be summed up as follows.

- It is distinguished from the regulation by being of individual applicability: the persons to whom it is addressed must be named in it and are the only ones bound by it. This requirement is met if, at the time

2 and 3 December 1985, Luxembourg.
On the sidelines of the European Council, federalist Europeans
demonstrate in favour of the European Union and of the
abolition of borders, which would not be applied between
certain countries until 10 years later.

the decision is issued, the category of addressees can be identified and can thereafter not be extended. Reference is made to the actual content of the decision, which must be such as to have a direct, individual impact on the citizen's situation. Even a third party may fall within the definition if, by reason of personal qualities or circumstances that distinguish them from others, they are individually affected and are identifiable as such in the same way as the addressee.

- ■ It is distinguished from the directive in that it is binding in its entirety (whereas the directive simply sets out the objective to be attained).

- ■ It is directly binding on those to whom it is addressed. A decision addressed to a Member State may in fact have the same direct effect in relation to the citizen as a directive.

RECOMMENDATIONS AND OPINIONS

A final category of legal measures explicitly provided for in the Treaties is recommendations and opinions. They enable the Union institutions to express a view to Member States, and in some cases to individual citizens, which is not binding and does not place any legal obligation on the addressee.

In recommendations, the party to whom they are addressed is called on, but not placed under any legal obligation, to behave in a particular way. For example, in cases where the adoption or amendment of a legal or administrative provision in a Member State causes a distortion of competition in the European internal market, the Commission may recommend to the State concerned such measures as are appropriate to avoid this distortion (Article 117(1), second sentence, TFEU).

Opinions, on the other hand, are issued by the Union institutions when giving an assessment of a given situation or developments in the Union or individual Member States. In some cases, they also prepare the way for subsequent, legally binding acts, or are a prerequisite for the institution of proceedings before the Court of Justice (Articles 258 and 259 TFEU).

The real significance of recommendations and opinions is political and moral. In providing for legal acts of this kind, the drafters of the Treaties anticipated that, given the authority of the Union institutions and their broader view and wide knowledge of conditions beyond the narrower national framework, those concerned would voluntarily comply with recommendations addressed to them and would react appropriately to the Union institutions' assessment of a particular situation. However, recommendations and opinions can have indirect legal effect where they are a preliminary to subsequent mandatory instruments or where the issuing institution has committed itself, thus generating legitimate expectations that must be met.

RESOLUTIONS, DECLARATIONS AND ACTION PROGRAMMES

Alongside the legal acts provided for in the Treaties, the Union institutions also have available a variety of other forms of action for forming and shaping the EU legal order. The most important of these are resolutions, declarations and action programmes.

Resolutions: These may be issued by the European Council, the Council and the European Parliament. They set out jointly held views and intentions regarding the overall process of integration and specific tasks within and outside the EU. Resolutions relating to the internal working of the EU are concerned, for example, with basic questions regarding political union, regional policy, energy policy and economic and monetary union (particularly the European Monetary System). The primary significance of these resolutions is that they help to give the future work of the Council a political direction. As manifestations of a commonly held political will, resolutions make it considerably easier to achieve a consensus in the Council, in addition to which they guarantee at least a minimum degree of correlation between decision-making hierarchies in the Community and the Member States. Any assessment of their legal significance must also take account of these functions, i.e. they should remain a flexible instrument and not be tied down by too many legal requirements and obligations.

Declarations: There are two different kinds of declaration. If a declaration is concerned with the further development of the Union, such as the Declaration on the EU, the Declaration on Democracy and the Declaration on Fundamental Rights and Freedoms, it is more or less equivalent to a resolution. Declarations of this type are mainly used to reach a wide audience or a specific group of addressees. The other type of declaration is issued in the context of the Council's decision-making process and sets out the views of all or individual Council members regarding the interpretation of the Council's decisions. Interpretative declarations of this kind are standard practice in the Council and are an essential means of achieving compromises. Their legal significance should be assessed under the basic principles of interpretation, according to which the key factor when interpreting the meaning of a legal provision should in all cases be the underlying intention of its originator. This principle is only valid, however, if the declaration receives the necessary public attention; this is because, for example, secondary Union legislation granting direct rights to individuals cannot be restricted by secondary agreements that have not been made public.

Action programmes: These programmes are drawn up by the Council and the Commission on their own initiative or at the instigation of the European Council and serve to put into practice the legislative programmes and general objectives laid down in the Treaties. If a programme is specifically provided for in the Treaties, the Union institutions are bound by those provisions when planning it. In the Union, these programmes are published in the form of White Papers. On the other hand, other programmes are in practice merely regarded as general guidelines with no legally binding effect. They are, however, an indication of the Union institutions' intended actions. Such programmes are published in the Union as Green Papers.

PUBLICATION AND COMMUNICATION

Legislative acts in the form of regulations, directives addressed to all Member States and decisions which do not specify to whom they are addressed are published in the *Official Journal of the European Union* (Series L = Legislation). They enter into force on the date specified in them or, if no date is specified, on the 20th day following their publication.

Non-legislative acts adopted in the form of regulations, directives or decisions, when the latter do not specify to whom they are addressed, are signed by the President of the institution which adopted them. They are published in the Official Journal (Series C = Communication).

Other directives, and decisions which specify to whom they are addressed, are notified to those to whom they are addressed and take effect upon such notification.

There is no obligation to publish and communicate non-binding instruments, but they are usually also published in the Official Journal ('Notices').

THE LEGISLATIVE PROCESS IN THE EU

Whereas in a state the will of the people will usually be expressed in parliament, it was for a long time the representatives of the Member States' governments meeting in the Council who played the decisive role in expressing the will of the EU. This was simply because the EU does not consist of a 'European nation' but owes its existence and form to the combined input of its Member States. These did not simply transfer part of their sovereignty to the EU, but pooled it on the understanding that they would retain the joint power to exercise it. However, as the process of Union integration has developed and deepened, this division of powers in the EU decision-making process, originally geared towards the defence of national interests by the Member States, has evolved into something much more balanced, with constant enhancement of the status of the European Parliament. The original procedure whereby Parliament was merely consulted was first of all broadened to include cooperation with the Council, and Parliament was eventually given powers of co-decision in the EU's legislative process.

Under the Treaty of Lisbon these co-decision powers of the Parliament became the 'ordinary legislative procedure', i.e. 'the general rule', thereby further enhancing the EU's democratic credentials. The co-decision procedure consists in the joint adoption by the European Parliament and the Council of a regulation, directive or decision on a proposal from the Commission. Only in a few explicit cases does the adoption of a regulation, directive or decision by the European Parliament with the participation of the Council, or by the latter with the participation of the European Parliament, constitute a special legislative procedure. In addition to these legislative procedures, there are also the 'approval procedure', which gives the European Parliament the final decision on the entry into force of a legal instrument, and the 'simplified procedure', which is used when non-binding instruments are issued by only one Union institution.

Course of the procedure

Formulation stage

The machinery is, in principle, set in motion by the Commission, which draws up a proposal for the Union measure to be taken (known as the 'right of initiative'). The proposal is prepared by the Commission department

ORDINARY LEGISLATIVE PROCEDURE (ARTICLE 294 TFEU)

COMMISSION

Proposals

COMMITTEE OF THE REGIONS | **EUROPEAN PARLIAMENT** *(first reading)* | **EUROPEAN ECONOMIC AND SOCIAL COMMITTEE**

Parliament position and Opinion of the Committees

COUNCIL
(first reading)

No amendments by Parliament or approval of all amendments by the Council **Instrument adopted** | *otherwise* | Position of the Council

EUROPEAN PARLIAMENT
(second reading)

Approval of Council's position | Amendments by majority of Members | Rejection of Council's position by majority of Members

Adopted in the wording which corresponds to the position of the Council | End of the legislative process Instrument is not adopted

COMMISSION

Approves Parliament's amendments | **Rejects Parliament's amendments**

COUNCIL
(second reading)

Approval of the amendments by qualified majority **Adoption of act** | Amendments rejected by Council | Approval of the amendments by unanimity **Adoption of act**

CONCILIATION COMMITTEE CONVENED BY THE COUNCIL/ PARLIAMENT

Agreement **Outcome confirmed at *third reading* by Council and Parliament** | No agreement **Instrument deemed rejected End of the legislative process** dealing with the particular field; frequently the department will also consult national experts at this stage. This sometimes takes the form of deliberations in specially convened committees; alternatively, experts may have questions put to them by the relevant departments of the Commission. However, the Commission is not obliged to accept the advice of the national experts when drawing up its proposals. The draft drawn up by the Commission, setting out the content and form of the measure to the last detail, goes before the Commission as a whole, when a simple majority is sufficient to have it adopted. It is now a 'Commission proposal' and is sent simultaneously to the Council and the European Parliament and, where consultation is required, to the European Economic and Social Committee and the Committee of the Regions, with detailed explanatory remarks.

First reading in Parliament and in the Council

The President of the European Parliament passes the proposal on to a Parliamentary coordination committee for further consideration. The outcome of the committee's deliberations is discussed at a plenary session of Parliament, and is set out in an opinion which may accept or reject the proposal or propose amendments. Parliament then sends its position to the Council.

The Council can now act as follows in the first reading.

- If it approves Parliament's position, the act is adopted in the form of that position; this marks the end of the legislative process.

- If the Council does not approve Parliament's position, it adopts its position at first reading and communicates it to the European Parliament.

The Council informs the European Parliament fully of the reasons which led it to adopt its position. The Commission informs the European Parliament fully of its position.

Second reading in Parliament and in the Council

The European Parliament has three months starting from the communication of the Council's position to do one of the following:

(1) approve the Council's position or not take a decision; the act concerned is then deemed to have been adopted in the wording which corresponds to the position of the Council;

(2) reject, by a majority of its component members, the Council's posi-tion; the proposed act is then deemed not to have been adopted and the legislative process ends;

(3) make, by a majority of its members, amendments to the Council's position; the text thus amended is then forwarded to the Council and to the Commission, which delivers an opinion on those amendments.

The Council discusses the amended position and has three months from the date of receiving Parliament's amendments to do one of the following.

(1) It can approve all of Parliament's amendments; the act in question is then deemed to have been adopted. A qualified majority is sufficient if the Commission is also in agreement with the amendments; if not, the Council can approve Parliament's amendments only by unanimity.

(2) It can choose not to approve all Parliament's amendments or it does not attain the required majority; this results in a conciliation procedure.

Conciliation procedure

The conciliation procedure is initiated by the President of the Council in agreement with the President of the European Parliament. At its heart is the Conciliation Committee, which is currently composed of 27 representa-tives each from the Council and the European Parliament. The Conciliation Committee has the task of reaching agreement on a joint text by a qualified majority within six weeks of its being convened, on the basis of the positions of the European Parliament and the Council at second reading.

The Commission takes part in the Conciliation Committee's proceedings and takes all the necessary initiatives with a view to reconciling the positions of the European Parliament and the Council.

If, within six weeks of its being convened, the Conciliation Committee does not approve the joint text, the proposed act is deemed not to have been adopted.

Third reading in Parliament and in the Council

If, within the six-week period, the Conciliation Committee approves a joint text, the European Parliament, acting by a majority of the votes cast, and the

Council, acting by a qualified majority, each have a period of six weeks from that approval in which to adopt the act in question in accordance with the joint text. If they fail to do so, the proposed act is deemed not to have been adopted and the legislative process is ended.

Publication

The final text (in the 23 current official languages of the Union: Bulgarian, Czech, Danish, Dutch, English, Estonian, Finnish, French, German, Greek, Hungarian, Irish, Italian, Latvian, Lithuanian, Maltese, Polish, Portuguese, Romanian, Slovak, Slovenian, Spanish and Swedish) is signed by the Presidents of the European Parliament and the Council, and then published in the *Official Journal of the European Union* or, if it is addressed to a specific group, notified to those to whom it is addressed.

The co-decision procedure represents both a challenge and an opportunity for Parliament. If the procedure is to operate successfully, there must be an agreement in the Conciliation Committee. However, the procedure also radically changes the relationship between Parliament and the Council. The two institutions are now placed on an equal footing in the legislative process, and it is up to Parliament and the Council to demonstrate their capacity for compromise and to direct their energies in the Conciliation Committee towards coming to an agreement.

APPROVAL PROCEDURE

Another principal form of Parliamentary involvement in the legislative process is the approval procedure, whereby a legal instrument can only be adopted with the prior approval of Parliament. This procedure does not, however, give Parliament any scope for directly influencing the nature of the legal provisions. For example, it cannot propose any amendments or secure their acceptance during the approval procedure; its role is restricted to accepting or rejecting the legal instrument submitted to it.

Provision is made for this procedure in connection with the accession of new Member States, the conclusion of association agreements, agreements with important budgetary implications for the EU and agreements with non-member countries in policy areas to which the ordinary legislative procedure applies (Article 218(6) TFEU).

SIMPLIFIED PROCEDURE

Under the simplified procedure, no Commission proposal is needed to initiate the legislative process.

This procedure applies to measures within the Commission's own powers (such as approval of state aid).

The simplified procedure is also used for the adoption of non-binding instruments, especially recommendations and opinions issued by the Commission or the Council. The Commission is not restricted to what is expressly provided for in the Treaties, but can also formulate recommendations and deliver opinions where it considers it necessary.

In the simplified procedure, legal acts are adopted by simple majority.

THE EU SYSTEM OF LEGAL PROTECTION

A Union which aspires to be a community governed by law must provide its citizens with a complete and effective system of legal protection. The European Union's system of legal protection meets this requirement. It recognises the right of the individual to effective judicial protection of the rights derived from EU law. This protection is one of the fundamental legal principles resulting from the constitutional traditions common to the Member States and the European Convention on Human Rights (Articles 6 and 13) and guaranteed by the EU's legal system (Court of Justice, General Court and the specialised courts). For this purpose a series of procedures is available, as described below.

TREATY INFRINGEMENT PROCEEDINGS (ARTICLE 258 TFEU)

This is a procedure for establishing whether a Member State has failed to fulfil an obligation imposed on it by Union law. It is conducted exclusively before the Court of Justice of the European Union. Given the seriousness of the accusation, the referral to the Court of Justice must be preceded by a preliminary procedure in which the Member State is given the opportunity to submit its observations. If the dispute is not settled at that stage, either the Commission (Article 258 TFEU) or another Member State (Article 259 TFEU) may institute an action in the Court. In practice the initiative is usually taken by the Commission. The Court investigates the complaint and decides whether a Treaty has been infringed. If so, the offending Member State is then required to take the measures needed to conform. If a Member State fails to comply with a judgment given against it, the Commission has the possibility of a second court ruling ordering that State to pay a lump-sum fine or a penalty (Article 260 TFEU). There are therefore serious financial implications for a Member State which continues to disregard a Court judgment against it for Treaty infringement.

ACTIONS FOR ANNULMENT (ARTICLE 263 TFEU)

Actions for annulment are a means to objective judicial control of the action of the Union institutions and bodies (abstract judicial review) and provide the citizen with access to EU justice, although with some restrictions (guarantee of individual legal protection).

They can be lodged against all measures of the Union institutions and bodies which produce binding legal effects likely to affect the interests of the applicant by seriously altering their legal position. In addition to the Member States, the European Parliament, the Council, the Commission, the Court of Auditors, the European Central Bank and the Committee of the Regions may also lodge actions for annulment provided that they invoke violation of the rights conferred on them.

Citizens and undertakings, on the other hand, can only proceed against decisions that are personally addressed to them or, though addressed to others, have a direct individual effect on them. This is deemed by the Court of Justice to be the case if a person is affected in so specific a way that a clear distinction exists between him or her and other individuals or undertakings. This criterion of 'immediacy' is intended to ensure that a matter is only referred to the Court of Justice or the General Court if the fact of the plaintiff's legal position being adversely affected is clearly established along with the nature of those adverse effects. The 'individual concern' requirement is also intended to prevent 'relator suits' from being filed.

If the action succeeds, the Court of Justice or General Court may declare the instrument void with retroactive effect. In certain circumstances, it may declare it void solely from the date of the judgment. However, in order to safeguard the rights and interests of those bringing legal actions, the declaration of nullity may be exempted from any such restriction.

COMPLAINTS FOR FAILURE TO ACT (ARTICLE 265 TFEU)

This form of action supplements the legal protection available against the European Parliament, the European Council, the Council, the Commission and the European Central Bank. There is a preliminary procedure whereby the complainant must first put the institution on notice to fulfil its duty. The order sought in an action by the institutions is a declaration that the body concerned has infringed the Treaty by neglecting to take a decision required of it. Where the action is brought by a citizen or an undertaking, it is for a declaration that the institution has infringed the Treaty by neglecting to address an individual decision to them. The judgment simply finds that the neglect was unlawful. The Court of Justice/General Court has no jurisdiction to order that a decision be taken: the party against whom judgment is given is merely required to take measures to comply with the judgment (Article 266 TFEU).

ACTIONS FOR DAMAGES (ARTICLES 268 AND 340(2) TFEU)

Citizens and undertakings — and also Member States — that sustain damage by reason of a fault committed by EU staff have the possibility to file actions for damages with the Court of Justice. The basis for EU liability is not fully set out by the Treaties and is otherwise governed by the general principles common to the laws of the Member States. The Court has fleshed this out, holding that the following conditions must be satisfied before an award of damages can be made: (1) there must be an unlawful act by a Union institution or by a member of its staff in the exercise of his or her functions. An unlawful act takes place when there is a serious infringement of a rule of Union law which confers rights on an individual, undertaking or Member State or has been passed to protect them. Laws recognised to have a protective nature are in particular the fundamental rights and freedoms of the internal market or the fundamental principles of the protection of legitimate expectations and proportionality. The infringement is sufficiently serious if the institution concerned has exceeded the limits of its discretionary power to a considerable degree. The Court tends to gear its findings to the narrowness of the category of persons affected by the offending measure and the scale of the damage sustained, which must be in excess of the commercial risk that can be reasonably expected in the business sector concerned; (2) actual harm must have been suffered; (3) there must be a causal link between the act of the Union institution and the damage sustained; (4) intent or negligence do not have to be proved.

ACTIONS BY COMMUNITY STAFF (ARTICLE 270 TFEU)

Disputes between the EU and its staff members or their surviving family members arising from the employment relationship can also be brought before the Court of Justice. Jurisdiction for these actions lies with the specialised court for the civil service attached to the General Court.

DISPUTES OVER UNION PATENTS (ARTICLES 257 AND 262 TFEU)

The legal basis for the establishment of a Union Patent Court was introduced by the Treaty of Nice. The Union Patent Court, which is yet to be created and will be located at the Court of Justice, would have jurisdiction concerning disputes over the future Union patent system. In particular, it would deal with proceedings relating to the infringement and validity of Union patents. The creation of the Union patent system itself aims to make it cheaper and easier to protect new inventions in all EU Member States, by means of a single procedure. It will thus remove competitive disadvantages suffered by Europe's innovators and stimulate investment in research and development.

APPEALS PROCEDURE (ARTICLE 256(2) TFEU)

The relationship between the Court of Justice and the General Court is designed in such a way that judgments of the General Court are subject to a right of appeal to the Court of Justice on points of law only. The appeal may lie on the grounds of lack of competence of the General Court, a breach of procedure which adversely affects the interests of the appellant or the infringement of Union law by the General Court. If the appeal is justified and procedurally admissible, the judgment of the General Court is rescinded by the Court of Justice. If the matter is ripe for a court ruling, the Court of Justice may issue its own judgment; otherwise, it must refer the matter back to the General Court, which is bound by the Court of Justice's legal assessment.

A similar system now exists between between the specialised courts and the General Court, with the General Court examining the decisions of the specialised courts as a sort of court of appeal. The (appellate) decision of the General Court can, in turn, be re-examined by the Court of Justice, although only under special circumstances.

PROVISIONAL LEGAL PROTECTION (ARTICLES 278 AND 279 TFEU)

Actions filed with the Court of Justice or the General Court, or appeals lodged against their judgments, do not have suspensive effect. It is, however, possible to apply to the Court of Justice or the General Court for an order to suspend the application of the contested act (Article 278 TFEU) or for an interim court order (Article 279 TFEU).

The merits of any application for interim measures are assessed by the courts on the basis of the following three criteria: (1) prospect of success on the main issue (*fumus boni juris*): this is assessed by the court in a preliminary summary examination of the arguments submitted by the appellant; (2) urgency of the order: this is assessed on the basis of whether the order applied for by the appellant is necessary in order to ward off serious and irreparable harm; the criteria used for making this assessment include the nature and seriousness of the infringement, and its specific and irreversibly adverse effects on the appellant's property and other objects of legal protection; financial loss is deemed to be of a serious and irreparable nature only if it cannot be made good even if the appellant is successful in the main proceedings; (3) weighing of interests: the adverse effects likely to be suffered by the appellant if the application for an interim order is refused are weighed against the EU's interest in immediate implementation of the measure, and against the detrimental effects on third parties if the interim order were to be issued.

PRELIMINARY RULINGS (ARTICLE 267 TFEU)

This is the procedure whereby the national courts can seek guidance on Union law from the Court of Justice. Where a national court is required to apply provisions of Union law in a case before it, it may stay the proceedings and ask the Court of Justice for clarification as to the validity of the Union instrument at issue and/or the interpretation of the instrument and of the Treaties. The Court of Justice responds in the form of a judgment rather than an advisory opinion; this emphasises the binding nature of its ruling. The preliminary ruling procedure, unlike the other procedures under consideration here, is not a contentious procedure but simply one stage in the proceedings that begin and end in the national courts.

The object is to secure a uniform interpretation of Union law and hence the unity of the EU legal order. Alongside the latter function, the procedure is also of importance in protecting individual rights. The national courts can only assess the compatibility of national and Union law and, in the event of any incompatibility, enforce Union law — which takes precedence and is directly applicable — if the content and scope of Union provisions are clearly set out. This clarity can normally only be brought about by a preliminary ruling from the Court of Justice, which means that proceedings for such a ruling offer Union citizens an opportunity to challenge actions of their own Member State which are in contravention of EU law and ensure enforcement of Union law before the national courts. This dual function of preliminary ruling proceedings compensates to a certain extent for the restrictions on individuals directly filing actions before the Court of Justice and is thus crucial for the legal protection of the individual. However, success in these proceedings depends ultimately on how 'keen' national judges and courts are to refer cases to a higher authority.

Subject matter: The Court of Justice rules on the interpretation of instruments of Union law and examines the validity of the Union institutions' acts of legal significance. Provisions of national law may not be the subject of a preliminary ruling. In proceedings for a preliminary ruling, the Court of Justice is not empowered to interpret national law or assess its compatibility with Union law. This fact is often overlooked in the questions referred to the Court of Justice, which is called on to look at many questions specifically concerned with the compatibility of provisions of national and Union law, or to decide on the applicability of a specific provision of Union law in proceedings pending before a national court. Although these questions are in fact procedurally inadmissible, the Court of Justice does not simply refer them back to the national court; instead, it reinterprets the question referred to it as a request by the referring court for basic or essential criteria for interpreting the Union legal provisions concerned, thus enabling the national court to then give its own assessment of compatibility between national and Union law. The procedure adopted by the Court of Justice is to extract from the documentation submitted — particularly the grounds for referral — those elements of Union law which need to be interpreted for the purpose of the underlying legal dispute.

Capacity to proceed: The procedure is available to all 'courts of the Member States'. This expression should be understood within the meaning of Union law and focuses not on the name but rather on the function and position occupied by a judicial body within the systems of legal protection in the Member States. On this basis, 'courts' are understood to mean all independent institutions (i.e. not subject to instructions) empowered to settle disputes in a constitutional state under due process of law. According to this definition, the constitutional courts in the Member States and dispute-settling authorities outside the state judicial system — but not private arbitration tribunals — are also entitled to refer cases. The national court's decision whether or not to make a reference will depend on the relevance of the point of Community law in issue for the settlement of the dispute before it, which is a matter for the national court to assess. The parties can only request, not require, it to refer a case. The Court of Justice considers the relevance of the point solely in terms of whether the question concerned is amenable to referral (i.e. whether it actually concerns the interpretation of the Union Treaties or the legal validity of an act by a Union institution) or whether a genuine legal dispute is involved (i.e. whether the questions on which the Court of Justice is to give its legal opinion in a preliminary ruling are merely hypothetical or relate to a point of law that has already been settled). It is exceptional for the Court to decline to consider a matter for these reasons because, given the special importance of cooperation between judicial authorities, the Court exercises restraint when applying these criteria. Nevertheless, recent judgments of the Court show that it has become more stringent as regards eligibility for referral in that it is very particular about the already established requirement that the order for referral contain a sufficiently clear and detailed explanation of the factual and legal background to the original proceedings, and that if this information is not provided it declares itself unable to give a proper interpretation of Union law and rejects the application for a preliminary ruling as inadmissible.

Obligation to refer: A national court or tribunal against whose decision there is no judicial remedy in national law is obliged to refer. The concept of right of appeal encompasses all forms of legal redress by which a court ruling may be reviewed in fact and in law (appeal) or only in law (appeal on points of law). The concept does not, however, encompass ordinary legal remedies with limited and specific effects (e.g. new proceedings, constitutional complaint). A court obliged to refer a case may only avoid such referral if the question is of no material importance for the outcome of the case before it or has already been answered by the Court of Justice or the interpretation of Union law is not open to reasonable doubt. However, the obligation to refer is unconditional where the validity of a Union instrument is at issue. The Court of Justice made it quite clear in this respect that it alone has the power to reject illegal provisions of Union law. The national courts must therefore apply and comply with Union law until it is declared invalid by the Court of Justice. A special arrangement applies to courts in proceedings for the granting of provisional legal protection. According to recent judgments of the Court of Justice, these courts are empowered, subject to certain conditions, to suspend enforcement of a national administrative act deriving from a Union regulation, or to issue interim orders in order to provisionally determine the arrangements of legal relations while disregarding an existing provision of Union law.

Failure to discharge the obligation to refer constitutes an infringement of the Union Treaties, which may make the Member State concerned liable to infringement proceedings. In practice, however, the effects of such a course of action are very limited, given that the government of the Member State concerned cannot comply with any order issued by the Court of Justice because the independence of its judiciary and the principle of separation of powers mean that it is unable to give instructions to national courts. Now that the principle of Member States' liability under Union law for failure to comply with it has been recognised (see next heading), the possibility of individuals filing for damages which may have arisen from the Member State concerned failing to meet its obligation to refer offers better prospects of success.

Effect: The preliminary ruling, issued in the form of a court order, is directly binding on the referring court and all other courts hearing the same case. In practice it also has a very high status as a precedent for subsequent cases of a like nature.

LIABILITY OF THE MEMBER STATES FOR INFRINGEMENTS OF UNION LAW

The liability of a Member State for harm suffered by individuals as a result of an infringement of Union law attributable to that State was established in principle by the Court of Justice in its judgment of 5 March 1996 in Joined

Cases C-46/93 *Brasserie du pêcheur* and C-48/93 *Factortame*. This was a precedent-setting judgment on a par with earlier Court judgments on the primacy of Union law, the direct applicability of provisions of Union law and recognition of the Union's own set of fundamental rights. The judgment is even referred to by the Court itself it as 'the necessary corollary of the direct effect of the Community provisions whose breach caused the damage sustained', and considerably enhances the possibilities for an individual to force State bodies of all three centres of power (i.e. legislative, executive and judiciary) to comply with and implement Union law. The judgment is a further development of the Court's rulings in *Francovich* and *Bonifaci*. Whilst the earlier judgments restricted the liability of the Member States to instances where individuals suffered harm as a result of failure to transpose in good time a directive granting them personal rights but not directly addressed to them, the latest judgment established the principle of general liability encompassing any infringement of Union law attributable to a Member State.

MEMBER STATES' LIABILITY FOR LEGAL ACTS OR FAILURE TO ACT

This form of liability is defined by three criteria which are largely the same as those applying to the Union in a similar situation.

(1) The aim of the Union provision which has been infringed must be to grant rights to the individual.

(2) The infringement must be sufficiently serious, i.e. a Member State must clearly have exceeded the limits of its discretionary powers to a considerable degree. This must be decided on by the national courts, which have sole responsibility for ascertaining the facts and assessing the seriousness of the infringements of Union law. The Court of Justice's judgment nevertheless offers the national courts a number of basic guidelines:

'The factors which the competent court may take into consideration include the clarity and precision of the rule breached, the measure of discretion left by that rule to the national or Community authorities, whether the infringement and the damage caused was intentional or involuntary, whether any error of law was excusable or inexcusable, the fact that the position taken by a Community institution may have contributed towards the omission, and the adoption of retention of national measures or practices contrary to Community law. On any view, a breach of Community law will clearly be sufficiently serious if it has persisted despite a judgment finding the infringement in question to be established, or a preliminary ruling or settled case-law of the Court on the matter from which it is clear that the conduct in question constituted an infringement.'

(3) A direct causal link must exist between the infringement of the obligation on the Member State and the harm suffered by the injured party. It is not necessary to demonstrate fault (intent or negligence) in addition to establishing that a sufficiently serious infringement of Union law has occurred.

LIABILITY FOR INFRINGEMENT OF UNION LAW BY THE COURTS

The Court of Justice makes it quite clear that the principles established by it for determining liability also apply to the last of the three central powers, namely the judiciary. Its judgments are now not only subject to review at the successive stages of appeal; if they were delivered in disregard or infringement of Union law, they may also be the subject of an action for damages before the competent courts in the Member States. When ascertaining the facts surrounding a judgment's infringement of Union law, proceedings of this kind must also reconsider the questions relating to the substance of Union law, in the process of which the court concerned may not merely invoke the binding effects of the judgment of the specialised court to which the case is referred. The court to which the competent national courts would have to refer questions of interpretation and/or the validity of Union provisions, and also the compatibility of national liability regimes with Union law, is again the Court of Justice, to which questions may be referred under the preliminary ruling procedure (Article 267 TFEU).

However, liability for infringement through a judgment will remain the exception. In view of the strict conditions attached, liability can be considered only if a court deliberately disregards Union law or, as in the *Köbler* case, a court of last instance, in violation of Union law, gives legal force to a decision to the detriment of the individual without having previously asked the Court of Justice to clarify the situation with regard to Union law which is relevant to the decision. In this latter case, it is essential for the protection of the rights of Union citizens who invoke Union law that the damage caused to them by a court of last instance be made good.

The position of Union law in relation to the legal order as a whole

After all that we have learnt about the structure of the EU and its legal set-up, it is not easy to assign Union law its rightful place in the legal order as a whole and define the boundaries between it and other legal orders. Two possible approaches to classifying it must be rejected from the outset. Union law must not be conceived of as a mere collection of international agreements, nor can it be viewed as a part of, or an appendage to, national legal systems.

AUTONOMY OF THE EU LEGAL ORDER

By establishing the Union, the Member States have limited their legislative sovereignty and in so doing have created a self-sufficient body of law that is binding on them, their citizens and their courts.

One of the best-known cases heard in the Court of Justice was *Costa* v *ENEL* in 1964, in which Mr Costa filed an action against the nationalisation of electricity generation and distribution, and the consequent vesting of the business of the former electricity companies in ENEL, the new public corporation.

The autonomy of the EU legal order is of fundamental significance for the nature of the EU, for it is the only guarantee that Union law will not be watered down by interaction with national law, and that it will apply uniformly throughout the Union. This is why the concepts of Union law are interpreted in the light of the aims of the EU legal order and of the Union in general. This Union-specific interpretation is indispensable, since particular rights are secured by Union law and without it they would be endangered, for each Member State could then, by interpreting provisions in different ways, decide individually on the substance of the freedoms that Union law is supposed to guarantee. An example is the concept of a 'worker', on which the scope of the concept of freedom of movement is based. The specific Union concept of the worker is quite capable of deviating from the concepts that are known and applied in the legal orders of the Member States. Furthermore, the only standard by which Union legal instruments are measured is Union law itself, and not national legislation or constitutional law.

Against the backdrop of this concept of the autonomy of the EU legal order, what is the relationship between Union law and national law?

Even if Union law constitutes a legal order that is self-sufficient in relation to the legal orders of the Member States, this situation must not be regarded as one in which the EU legal order and the legal systems of the Member States are superimposed on one another like layers of bedrock. The fact that they are applicable to the same people, who thus simultaneously become citizens of a national State and of the EU, negates such a rigid demarcation of these legal orders. Secondly, such an approach disregards the fact that Union law can become operational only if it forms part of the legal orders of the Member States. The truth is that the EU legal order and the national legal orders are interlocked and interdependent.

INTERACTION BETWEEN UNION LAW AND NATIONAL LAW

This aspect of the relationship between Union law and national law covers those areas where the two systems complement each other. Article 4(3) of the TEU is clear enough:

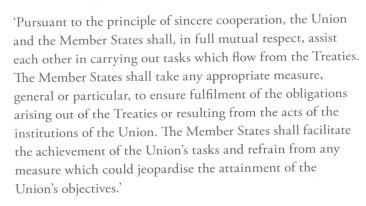

'Pursuant to the principle of sincere cooperation, the Union and the Member States shall, in full mutual respect, assist each other in carrying out tasks which flow from the Treaties. The Member States shall take any appropriate measure, general or particular, to ensure fulfilment of the obligations arising out of the Treaties or resulting from the acts of the institutions of the Union. The Member States shall facilitate the achievement of the Union's tasks and refrain from any measure which could jeopardise the attainment of the Union's objectives.'

This general principle of sincere cooperation was inspired by an awareness that the EU legal order on its own is not able to fully achieve the objectives pursued by the establishment of the EU. Unlike a national legal order, the EU legal order is not a self-contained system but relies on the support of the national systems for its operation. All three branches of government — legislature, executive and judiciary — therefore need to acknowledge that the EU legal order is not a 'foreign' system and that the Member States and the Union institutions have established indissoluble links between themselves so as to achieve their common objectives. The EU is not just a community of interests; it is a community based on solidarity. It follows that national authorities are required not only to observe the Union Treaties and secondary legislation; they must also implement them and bring them to life. The interaction between the two systems is so multifaceted that a few examples are called for.

The first illustration of how the EU and national legal orders mesh with and complement each other is the directive, already considered in the chapter on legislation. All the directive itself fixes in binding terms is the result to be achieved by the Member State; it is for national authorities, via domestic law, to decide how and by what means the result is actually brought about. In the judicial field, the two systems mesh through the preliminary ruling procedure referred to in Article 267 of the TFEU, whereby national courts may, or sometimes must, refer questions on the interpretation and validity of Union law to the Court of Justice, whose ruling may well be decisive in settling the dispute before them. Two things are clear: firstly, the courts in the Member States are required to observe and apply Union law; and secondly, the interpretation of Union law and declarations as to its validity are the sole preserve of the Court of Justice. The interdependence of EU and national law is further illustrated by what happens when gaps in EU law need to be filled: Union law refers back to existing rules of national law to complete the rules it itself determines. This principle applies to the full range of obligations under Union law unless the latter has laid down rules for its own enforcement. In any such case, national authorities enforce Union law by the provisions of their own legal systems. But the principle is subject to one proviso: the uniform application of Union law must be preserved, for it would be wholly unacceptable for citizens and undertakings to be judged by different criteria — and therefore be treated unjustly.

1 March 2004.
Woman drawing a chalk map of Europe as it would look at 1 January 2007.

Conflict between Union law and national law

However, the relationship between Union law and national law is also characterised by an occasional 'clash' or conflict between the Union legal order and the national legal orders. Such a situation always arises when a provision of Union law confers rights and imposes obligations directly upon Union citizens while its content conflicts with a rule of national law. Concealed behind this apparently simple problem area are two fundamental questions underlying the construction of the EU, the answers to which were destined to become the acid test for the existence of the EU legal order, namely the direct applicability of Union law and the primacy of Union law over conflicting national law.

DIRECT APPLICABILITY OF UNION LAW TO NATIONAL LAW

Firstly, the direct applicability principle simply means that Union law confers rights and imposes obligations directly not only on the Union institutions and the Member States but also on the Union's citizens.

One of the outstanding achievements of the Court of Justice is that it has enforced the direct applicability of Union law despite the initial resistance of certain Member States, and has thus guaranteed the existence of the EU legal order. Its case-law on this point started with a case already mentioned, namely that of the Dutch transport firm *Van Gend & Loos*. The firm brought an action in a Dutch court against the Dutch customs authorities, which had charged increased customs duties on a chemical product imported from the Federal Republic of Germany. In the final analysis, the outcome of these proceedings depended on the question of whether individuals too may invoke Article 12 of the EEC Treaty, which specifically prohibits the introduction by the Member States of new customs duties and the increase of existing duties in the common market. Despite the advice of numerous governments and its Advocate General, the Court ruled that, in view of the nature and objective of the Union, the provisions of Union law were in all cases directly applicable. In the grounds for its judgment, the Court stated that:

> '... the Community constitutes a new legal order ... the subjects of which comprise not only the Member States but also their nationals. Independently of the legislation of Member States, Community law not only imposes obligations on individuals but

is also intended to confer upon them rights. These rights arise not only where they are expressly granted by the Treaty, but also by reason of obligations which the Treaty imposes in a clearly defined way upon individuals as well as upon the Member States and upon the institutions of the Community.'

That bald statement does not, however, get us very far, since the question remains as to which provisions of Union law are directly applicable. The Court first of all looked at this question in relation to primary Union legislation and declared that individuals may be directly subject to all the provisions of the Union Treaties which (i) set out absolute conditions, (ii) are complete in themselves and self-contained in legal terms and therefore (iii) do not require any further action on the part of the Member States or the Union institutions in order to be complied with or acquire legal effect.

The Court ruled that the former Article 12 EEC met these criteria, and that the firm Van Gend & Loos could therefore also derive rights from it which the court in the Netherlands was obliged to safeguard, as a consequence of which the Dutch court invalidated the customs duties levied in contravention of the Treaty. Subsequently, the Court continued to apply this reasoning in regard to other provisions of the EEC Treaty that are of far greater importance to citizens of the Union than Article 12. The judgments that are especially noteworthy here concern the direct applicability of provisions on freedom of movement (Article 45 TFEU), freedom of establishment (Article 49 TFEU) and freedom to provide services (Article 56 TFEU).

With regard to the guarantees concerning freedom of movement, the Court of Justice delivered a judgment declaring them directly applicable in the *Van Duyn* case. The facts of this case were as follows: Miss van Duyn, a Dutch national, was in May 1973 refused permission to enter the United Kingdom in order to take up employment as a secretary with the Church of Scientology, an organisation considered by the Home Office to be 'socially harmful'. Invoking the Union rules on freedom of movement for workers, Miss van Duyn brought an action before the High Court, seeking a ruling that she was entitled to stay in the United Kingdom for the purpose of employment and be given leave to enter the United Kingdom. In answer to a question referred by the High Court, the Court of Justice held that Article 48 of the EEC Treaty (Article 45 TFEU) was directly applicable and hence conferred on individuals rights that are enforceable before the courts of a Member State.

The Court of Justice was asked by the Belgian *Conseil d'État* to give a ruling on the direct applicability of provisions guaranteeing freedom of establishment. The Conseil d'État had to decide on an action brought by a Dutch lawyer, J. Reyners, who wished to assert his rights arising out of Article 52 of the EEC Treaty (Article 49 TFEU). Mr Reyners felt obliged to bring the action after he had been denied admission to the legal profession in Belgium because of his foreign nationality, despite the fact that he had passed the necessary Belgian examinations. In its judgment of 21 July 1974, the Court held that unequal treatment of nationals and foreigners as regards establishment could no longer be maintained, as Article 52 of the EEC Treaty had been directly applicable since the end of the transitional period and hence entitled Union citizens to take up and pursue gainful employment in another Member State in the same way as a national of that State. As a result of this judgment Mr Reyners had to be admitted to the legal profession in Belgium.

The Court of Justice was given an opportunity in the *Van Binsbergen* case to specifically establish the direct applicability of provisions relating to the freedom to provide services. These proceedings involved, among other things, the question of whether a Dutch legal provision to the effect that only persons habitually resident in the Netherlands could act as legal representatives before an appeal court was compatible with the Union rules on freedom to provide services. The Court ruled that it was not compatible on the grounds that all restrictions to which Union citizens might be subject by reason of their nationality or place of residence infringe Article 59 of the EEC Treaty (Article 56 TFEU) and are therefore void.

Also of considerable importance in practical terms is the recognition of the direct applicability of provisions on the free movement of goods (Article 41 TFEU), the principle of equal pay for men and women (Article 157 TFEU), the general prohibition of discrimination (Article 25 TFEU) and freedom of competition (Article 101 TFEU). As regards secondary legislation, the question of direct applicability only arises in relation to directives and decisions addressed to the Member States, given that regulations and decisions addressed to individuals already derive their direct applicability from the Union Treaties (Article 288(2) and (4) TFEU). Since 1970 the Court has extended its principles concerning direct applicability to provisions in directives and in decisions addressed to the Member States.

The practical importance of the direct effect of Union law in the form in which it has been developed and brought to fruition by the Court of Justice can scarcely be overemphasised. It improves the position of the individual by turning the freedoms of the common market into rights that may be enforced in a national court of law. The direct effect of Union law is therefore one of the pillars, as it were, of the EU legal order.

PRIMACY OF UNION LAW OVER NATIONAL LAW

The direct applicability of a provision of Union law leads to a second, equally fundamental question: what happens if a provision of Union law gives rise to direct rights and obligations for the Union citizen and thereby conflicts with a rule of national law?

Such a conflict between Union law and national law can be settled only if one gives way to the other. Union legislation contains no express provision on the question. None of the Union Treaties contains a provision stating, for example, that Union law overrides or is subordinate to national law. Nevertheless, the only way of settling conflicts between Union law and national law is to grant Union law primacy and allow it to supersede all national provisions that diverge from a Union rule and take their place in the national legal orders. After all, precious little would remain of the EU legal order if it were to be subordinated to national law. Union rules could be set aside by any national law. There would no longer be any question of the uniform and equal application of Union law in all Member States. Nor would the EU be able to perform the tasks entrusted to it by the Member States. The Union's ability to function would be jeopardised, and the construction of a united Europe on which so many hopes rest would never be achieved.

No such problem exists as regards the relationship between international law and national law. Given that international law does not become part of a country's own legal order until it is absorbed by means of an act of incorporation or transposition, the issue of primacy is decided on the basis of national law alone. Depending on the order of precedence ascribed to international law by a national legal system, it may take precedence over constitutional law, be ranked between constitutional law and ordinary statutory law, or merely have the same status as statutory law. The relationship between incorporated or transposed international law and national law is determined by applying the rule under which the most recently enacted legal provisions prevail against those previously in place (*lex posterior derogat legi priori*). These national rules on conflict of laws do not, however, apply to the relationship between Union law and national law, because Union law does not form part of any national legal order. Any conflict between Union law and national law may only be settled on the basis of the EU legal order.

Once again it fell to the Court of Justice, in view of these implications, to establish — despite opposition from several Member States — the principle of the primacy of Union law that is essential to the existence of the EU legal order. In so doing, it erected the second pillar of the EU legal order alongside direct applicability, which was to turn that legal order into a solid edifice at last.

In *Costa* v *ENEL*, the Court made two important observations regarding the relationship between Union law and national law.

- The Member States have definitively transferred sovereign rights to a Community created by them and subsequent unilateral measures would be inconsistent with the concept of EU law.

- It is a principle of the Treaty that no Member State may call into question the status of Union law as a system uniformly and generally applicable throughout the EU.

It follows from this that Union law, which was enacted in accordance with the powers laid down in the Treaties, has primacy over any conflicting law of the Member States. Not only is it stronger than earlier national law, but it also has a limiting effect on laws adopted subsequently.

Ultimately, the Court did not in its judgment call into question the nationalisation of the Italian electricity industry, but it quite emphatically established the primacy of Union law over national law.

The legal consequence of this rule of precedence is that, in the event of a conflict of laws, national law which is in contravention of Union law ceases to apply and no new national legislation may be introduced unless it is compatible with Union law.

The Court has since consistently upheld this finding and has, in fact, developed it further in one respect. Whereas the Costa judgment was concerned only with the question of the primacy of Union law over ordinary national laws, the Court confirmed the principle of primacy also with regard to the relationship between Union law and national constitutional law. After initial hesitation, national courts in principle accepted the interpretation of the Court of Justice. In the Netherlands, no difficulties could arise anyway, because the primacy of Treaty law over national statute law is expressly laid down in the constitution (Articles 65 to 67). In the other Member States, the principle of the primacy of Union law over national law has likewise been recognised by national courts. However, the constitutional courts of Germany and Italy initially refused to accept the primacy of Union law over national constitutional law, in particular regarding the guaranteed protection of fundamental rights. They withdrew their objections only after the protection of fundamental rights in the EU legal order had reached a standard that corresponded in essence to that of their national constitutions. However, Germany's Federal Constitutional Court continues to entertain misgivings about further integration, as it has made quite clear in its judgments on the Treaty of Maastricht and, more recently, the Treaty of Lisbon.

INTERPRETATION OF NATIONAL LAW IN LINE WITH UNION LAW

To prevent conflict between Union law and national law arising from the application of the rule of precedence, all State bodies that specifically implement or rule on the law can draw on the interpretation of national law in line with Union law.

It took a fairly long time for the concept of interpretation in line with EU law to be recognised by the Court of Justice and incorporated into the Union legal order. After the Court of Justice had initially considered it to be appropriate to ensure that national laws were in harmony with a directive only when requested to do so by national courts, it established an obligation to interpret national law in accordance with the directives for the first time in 1984 in the case *Von Colson and Kamann*. This case ruled on the amount of compensation to be awarded for discrimination against women with regard to access to employment. Whereas the relevant German legal provisions provided only for compensation for 'Vertrauensschaden' (futile reliance on a legitimate expectation), Directive 76/207/EEC states that national law must provide for effective penalties to ensure that equal opportunities are provided with regard to access to employment. Since, however, the relevant penalties were not set out in more detail, the directive could not be considered directly applicable on this point, and there was a risk that the Court of Justice would have to rule that, although the national law failed to comply with Union law, there was no basis for the national courts to not take the national law into account. The Court of Justice therefore ruled that the national courts were obliged to interpret and apply national legislation in civil matters in such a way that there were effective penalties for discrimination on the basis of gender. A purely symbolic compensation would not meet the requirement of an effective application of the directive.

The Court of Justice attributes the legal basis for the interpretation of national law in line with Union law to the general principle of sincere cooperation (Article 4(3) TEU). Under this article, Member States must take all appropriate measures, whether general or particular, to ensure fulfilment of the obligations arising out of the EU Treaty or resulting from action taken by the Union institutions. The national authorities are therefore also obliged to bring the interpretation and application of national law, which is secondary to Union law, into line with the wording and purpose of Union law (duty of cooperation). For the national courts, this is reflected in their role as European courts in the sense that they ensure the correct application and observance of Community law.

One particular form of interpretation of national law in accordance with Union law is that of interpretation in accordance with the directives, under which Member States are obliged to implement directives. Legal practitioners and courts must help their Member States to meet this obligation in full by applying the principle of interpretation in accordance with the directives. Interpretation of national law in accordance with the directives ensures that there is conformity with the directives at the level at which law is applied, and thus ensures that national implementing law is interpreted and applied uniformly in all Member States. This prevents matters from being differentiated at national level which have just been harmonised at Union level by means of the directive.

The limits of interpretation of national law in line with Community law are in the unambiguous wording of a national law which is not open to interpretation; even though there is an obligation under Community law to interpret national law in line with Union law, national law may not be interpreted 'contra legem'. This also applies in cases where the national legislator explicitly refuses to transpose a directive into national law. A resulting conflict between Union law and national law can be resolved only by means of proceedings against the Member State concerned for failure to fulfil obligations under the Treaty (Articles 258 and 259 TFEU).

27 September 1964, Brussels.
Car displaying a European registration plate parked in front of the
'Joyeuse entrée', building, the future headquarters of the European
Commission, which was under construction.

Conclusions

What overall picture emerges of the EU's legal order?

The EU's legal order is the true foundation of the Union, giving it a common system of law under which to operate. Only by creating new law and upholding it can the Union's underlying objectives be achieved. The EU legal order has already accomplished a great deal in this respect. It is thanks not least to this new legal order that the largely open borders, the substantial trade in goods and services, the migration of workers and the large number of transnational links between companies have already made the common market part of everyday life for some 500 million people. Another, historically important, feature of the Union legal order is its peacemaking role. With its objective of maintaining peace and liberty, it replaces force as a means of settling conflicts by rules of law that bind both individuals and the Member States into a single Community. As a result the Union legal order is an important instrument for the preservation and creation of peace.

The community of law of the EU and its underlying legal order can survive only if compliance with and safeguarding of that legal order are guaranteed by the two cornerstones: the direct applicability of Union law and the primacy of Union law over national law. These two principles, the existence and maintenance of which are resolutely upheld by the Court of Justice, guarantee the uniform and priority application of Union law in all Member States.

For all its imperfections, the EU legal order makes an invaluable contribution towards solving the political, economic and social problems of the Member States of the Union.

Annex

Nature and primacy of Union law

Case 26/62 *Van Gend & Loos* [1963] ECR 1 (nature of Union law; rights and obligations of individuals).

Case 6/64 *Costa* v *ENEL* [1964] ECR 1251 (nature of Union law; direct applicability, primacy of Union law).

Case 14/83 *Von Colson and Kamann* [1984] ECR 1891 (interpretation of national law in line with Union law).

Case C-213/89 *Factortame* [1990] ECR I-2433 (direct applicability and primacy of Union law).

Joined Cases C-6/90 and C-9/90 *Francovich and others* [1991] ECR I-5357 (effect of Union law; liability of Member States for failure to discharge Union obligations: non-transposal of a directive).

Joined Cases C-46/93 *and* C-48/93 *Brasserie du pêcheur* and *Factortame* [1996] ECR I-1029 (effect of Union law; general liability of Member States for failure to discharge Union obligations).

Joined Cases C-10/97 to C-22/97 *IN.CO.GE '90* [1998] ECR I-6307 (primacy of Union law).

Case C-416/00 *Morellato* [2003] ECR I-9343 (primacy of Union law).

Joined Cases C-397/01 to C-403/01 *Pfeiffer and others* [2004] ECR I-8835 (interpretation of national law in line with Union law).

Powers of the EU

Case 8/55 *Fédération charbonnière de Belgique* [1954–1956] ECR 292 (implied powers; official fixing of prices).

Case 22/70 *AETR* [1971] ECR 263 (legal personality and treaty-making powers of the EU).

Case 6/76 *Kramer* [1976] ECR 1279 (external relations; international commitments; authority of the EU).

Opinion 1/91 [1993] ECR I-6079 (EEA Agreement I; distribution of powers).

Opinion 2/91 [1993] ECR I-1061 (distribution of powers between the EU and the Member States).

Opinion 1/94 [1994] ECR I-5267 (WTO Agreement; distribution of powers).

Opinion 2/94 [1996] ECR I-1759 (accession by the EC to the ECHR; absence of powers).

Effects of legal acts

Case 2/74 *Reyners* [1974] ECR 631 (direct applicability; freedom of establishment).

Case 33/74 *van Binsbergen* [1974] ECR 1299 (direct applicability; provision of services).

Case 41/74 *Van Duyn* [1974] ECR 1337 (direct applicability; freedom of movement).

Case 11/77 *Patrick* [1977] ECR 1199 (direct applicability; right of establishment).

Case 70/83 *Kloppenburg* [1984] ECR 1075 (directives; direct applicability).

Case 152/84 *Marshall* [1986] ECR 723 (directives; direct applicability).

Case 103/88 *Costanzo* [1989] ECR 1861 (directives; direct applicability; conditions; consequences).

Case 322/88 *Grimaldi* [1989] ECR 4407 (recommendations; direct applicability or its absence; observance by national courts).

Case C-188/89 *Forster* [1990] ECR I-3343 (directives; horizontal direct effect).

Case C-292/89 *Antonissen* [1991] ECR I-773 (statements in Council minutes; status for interpretation purposes).

Case C-91/92 *Faccini Dori* [1994] ECR I-3325 (directives; horizontal direct effect).

Case C-431/92 *Commission* v *Germany* (Grosskotzenburg) [1995] ECR I-2189 (directive; effect of objective law).

Case C-465/93 *Atlanta Fruchthandelsgesellschaft* [1995] ECR I-3761 (examination of validity of a regulation; preliminary ruling; ordering of interim measures; conditions).

Case C-469/93 *Chiquita Italia* [1995] ECR I-4533 (direct effect of provisions of the GATT and the Lomé Convention).

Case C-368/96 *Generics* [1998] ECR I-7967 (statements in minutes; status for interpretation purposes).

Case C-144/01 *Mangold* [2005] ECR I-9981 (directive; horizontal direct effect).

Fundamental rights

Case 29/69 *Stauder* [1969] ECR 419 (fundamental rights; general principles of law).

Case 11/70 *Internationale Handelsgesellschaft* [1970] ECR 1125 (fundamental rights; general principles of law).

Cases 146/73 and 166/73 *Rheinmühlen I, II* [1974] ECR 33 and 139 (extent to which national courts are bound by rulings of higher courts).

Case 4/73 *Nold* [1974] ECR 491 (fundamental rights; general principles of law; common constitutional traditions).

Case 175/73 *Amalgamated European Public Service Union* [1974] ECR 917 (freedom to form associations).

Case 130/75 *Prais* [1976] ECR 1589 (freedom of religion and belief).

Case 149/77 *Defrenne* [1978] ECR 1381 (fundamental rights; general principles of law).

Case 44/79 *Hauer* [1979] ECR 3727 (fundamental rights; right of property).

Case 85/79 *Hoffmann-La Roche* [1979] ECR 461 (fundamental rights; principle of the right to be heard).

Case 293/83 *Gravier* [1985] ECR 593 (equal treatment; students' fees).

Case 234/85 *Keller* [1986] ECR 2897 (freedom to pursue a trade or profession).

Joined Cases 46/87 and 227/88 *Hoechst* [1989] ECR 2919 (fundamental rights; principle of the right to be heard; administrative procedure; inviolability of the home; reference to the ECHR).

Case 265/87 *Schräder* [1989] ECR 2263 (right of ownership; freedom to pursue a trade or profession; restrictions).

Case 5/88 *Wachauf* [1989] ECR 2633 (restrictions on fundamental rights).

Case C-219/91 *Ter Voort* [1992] ECR I-5485 (freedom of expression).

Case C-97/91 *Borelli* [1992] ECR I-6313 (fundamental rights; right to take action in the courts).

Case C-357/89 *Raulin* [1992] ECR I-1027 (equal treatment; prohibition of discrimination on grounds of nationality).

Case C-132/91 *Katsikas* [1992] ECR I-6577 (fundamental rights; freedom to pursue a trade or profession).

Case C-2/92 *Bostock* [1994] ECR I-955 (fundamental rights; right of ownership; freedom to pursue a trade or profession; observance when implementing EU law).

Case C-280/93 *Germany* v *Council* [1994] ECR I-5065 (right of ownership; freedom to pursue a trade or profession; restrictions in the public interest).

Case C-415/93 *Bosman and others* [1995] ECR I-4921 (fundamental rights; freedom to pursue a trade or profession).

Case C-55/94 *Gebhard* [1995] ECR I-4165 (fundamental rights; right of establishment; freedom to pursue a trade or profession).

Opinion 2/94 [1996] ECR I-1759 (fundamental rights; accession by the EU to the ECHR).

Case C-377/98 *Netherlands* v *Parliament and Council* [2001] ECR I-7079 (human dignity; right to physical integrity).

Case C-274/99 P, *Connolly* [2001] ECR I-1611 (freedom of opinion).

Case C-60/00 *Carpenter* [2002] ECR I-6279 (protection of the family).

Case C-112/00 *Schmidberger* [2003] ECR I-5659 (bounds of Community fundamental rights; freedom of assembly and freedom of opinion).

Case C-276/01 *Steffensen* [2003] ECR I-3735 (right to effective legal protection).

Case C-25/02 *Rinke* [2003] ECR I-8349 (general principle of equality).

Case C-36/02 *Omega* [2004] ECR I-9609 (bounds of fundamental rights).

GENERAL PRINCIPLES OF LAW (SELECTION)

Legal certainty

Joined Cases 18/65 and 35/65 *Gutmann* [1967] ECR 61.

Case 98/78 *Racke* [1979] ECR 69.

Case 96/78 *Decker* [1979] ECR 101.

Case 61/79 *Denkavit* [1980] ECR 1205.

Cases 66/79, 127/79 and 128/79 *Salumi* [1980] ECR 1237.

Case 70/83 *Kloppenburg* [1984] ECR 1075.

Joined Cases T-551/93 and T-231/94 to T-234/94 *Industrias Pesqueras Campos and Others* [1996] ECR II-247.

Joined Cases T-116/01 and T-118/01 *P & O European Ferries (Vizcaya)* v *Commission* [2003] ECR II-2957.

Proportionality

Case 116/76 *Granaria* [1977] ECR 1247.

Case 265/87 *Schräder* [1989] ECR 2237.

Case C-161/96 *Südzucker* [1998] ECR I-281.

Case C-171/03 *Toeters* [2004] ECR I-10945.

Protection of legitimate expectations

Case 74/74 *CNTA* [1975] ECR 533.

Case 120/86 *Mulder* [1988] ECR 2321.

Case 170/86 *Von Deetzen* [1988] ECR 2355.

Case C-368/89 *Crispoltoni I* [1991] ECR I-3695.

Case T-119/95 *Hauer* [1998] ECR II-2713.

Subsidiarity principle

Case T-29/92 *SPO* [1995] ECR II-289.

Case C-84/94 *United Kingdom* v *Council* [1996] ECR I-5755.

Joined Cases C-36/97 and C-37/97 *Kellinhusen and Ketelsen* [1998] ECR I-6337.

Case C-491/01 *British American Tobacco (Investments) and Imperial Tobacco* [2002] ECR I-11453.

Union citizenship

Case C-85/96 *Martínez Sala* [1998] ECR I-2691.

Case C-184/99 *Grzelczyk* [2001] ECR I-6193.

Case C-224/98 *d'Hoop* [2002] ECR I-6191.

Case C-413/99 *Baumbast* [2002] ECR I-7091.

Case C-403/03 *Schempp* [2005] ECR I-6421.

European Commission
The ABC of European Union law
by Professor Klaus-Dieter Borchardt

Luxembourg: Publications Office of the European Union, 2010

2010 — 131 pp. — 163 × 250 mm

ISBN 978-92-78-40525-0

doi:10.2830/13717